ONE
Salute Too Many

By

LISA HUNT

Based on a true story

Table of Contents

Dedicated to my daughter Arielle Rose
who fills me with inspiration every day

CHAPTER ONE

The Beginning

As the sun glistened in my eyes, it blinded me from seeing the blue sky ahead. My eyes became drawn to the reflection of a flag that blew along the ripples in the water. In a few steps, I would draw my right arm for the last time, creating an angle that means not only freedom but also pride.

"Permission to go ashore for the last time," I stated, each word pronounced with precision.

"Permission granted," spoke Petty Officer Somner as she rendered a salute in response to mine.

Despite her attempt to remain professional, she broke down and gave me a hug.

"Be lucky you are out of here. I still have a few more months," she said.

Looking back at her, I responded, "Time will go by fast, I hope." I always liked Somner. She had always been a friend to me and was one of the nicest on the ship.

As I walked away, I couldn't help but think back on all the memories, those both good and bad. It seemed like a dream.

My name is Lisa Taylor and this is my story.

It was May 15, 2007. On a cold and rainy night, I arrived at boot camp in Great Lakes, Illinois. As the bus pulled through the gate of the base, I thought about what I would experience next. Trust me. I had heard enough horror stories about the drill instructors boarding the bus to scream in people's faces. The night seemed quiet enough and most of the others were sound asleep. The ride to the base was relaxing. Even as we pulled in, I saw only two guards standing out in the rain. They flagged the bus driver to go ahead and he drove into the darkness. I noticed a large, beige building in the distance. As the bus came to a stop, the door opened and let in a cool breeze. Suddenly, the lights of the bus came on, making it hard for me to adjust my eyes. As I began to stand, two drill instructors boarded the bus and began screaming.

One of the drill instructors, a big, buff guy, screamed at the top of his lungs. "Get off the bus now! Hurry up!" The more he yelled, the redder his face became. His veins popped out of his neck and every time he yelled, cold drops of spit hit my face and arms.

The other drill instructor was a short, dark-haired, plump woman. She yelled, "Are you eyeballing me? Keep your eyes straight ahead when you get off the bus and stand in a single line."

I grabbed my bag and got off the bus and then I stood in line with the other recruits. I was not about to turn my head. I made sure to be as low-key as possible. The line began to move toward a large building with classrooms. More drill instructors circled the line and proceeded to yell. I felt like a cow being herded in a cattle drive. Standing inside the building, I must have looked at the person's head in front of me for a good twenty minutes. Why were we in such a hurry if all we were doing was standing in line? Anyone who has ever served in the military knows that the "hurry up and wait" motto always applies. That's exactly what we were doing. After twenty minutes, more navy personnel arrived and began breaking us up into groups. I was sent to the urinalysis group. As fun as the evening began, more fun was to come. We were placed in a circle and informed by the drill instructors that until we felt the need to urinate, we had to march in a circle. Every time we passed the drinking fountain, we had to take a drink. I don't know how many hours I marched in that circle before I underwent urinalysis. Not that it mattered. The recruits stayed up all night to do paperwork, receive recruit-blue sweats, and have blood drawn. As I finally felt the urge to urinate, I raised my arm to announce in front of everyone that I needed to use the head. The head is the bathroom. I only knew this because I'd heard them refer to it by that name all night. The woman taking the urinalysis handed me a small bottle and led me into a large room with a bunch of toilets. In the room with me, a handful of recruits were also trying to urinate. It is nearly impossible to go to the bathroom with a bunch of people watching. Squatting to urinate into a small bottle is not the most flattering picture. Luckily, I had to go pretty badly, so I really didn't care who saw me do what. I was in and out of there. Once I finished, I was led into a classroom to sit at a desk. One of the drill instructors asked the recruits questions, telling them what division they would be in. He came up to me and asked if I had any talents or hobbies. I told him that I played the violin and taught dance. He told me I would be in division 933, the flags division. This meant that I would participate in the graduation ceremonies making flag formations and marching.

Half asleep, I noticed a few chiefs and first classes coming into the classroom. They talked and laughed with the drill instructors that brought us in. When the room became quiet, a small, blond boatswain's mate (BM) 1 started screaming for the recruits from division 933 to line up outside the classroom door. For anyone who is not familer with the enlisted structure of the Navy, an E-1 to E-3 are seaman, E-4 petty officer 3rd class, E-5 petty officer 2nd class, E-6 petty officer 1st class, E-7 chief petty officer, E-8 senior chief petty officer, and an E-9 master chief petty officer. Jumping to my feet, I ran to get in line. Next to BM1, a very tall, stern-looking chief stood next to a bald guy with an operations specialist (OS)1 insignia on his sleeve. The insignia caught my eye since that was going to be my job.

Looking around at us, the chief rocked back and forth on his feet and then said, "All eyes should be forward, on the person in front of you. If I see anyone looking around, you will be giving me push-ups until I tell you to stop. We will be your instructors. You will answer yes, sir, no, sir, yes, ma'am, and no, ma'am." As I listened, I couldn't help but notice that he had a bad lisp. Though there's nothing wrong with having a lisp, it made it hard to take him seriously. He tried to act so tough, but he sounded like Daffy Duck.

Once we got to our barracks, we were issued racks and met our rack buddies. I had the top rack. A girl named Grant had the bottom rack. She seemed really nice. She had a southern accent with bright, red hair and freckles. As we sat in front of our racks with our legs crossed, the drill instructors issued everyone in the division their jobs. My job was to be part of "the dirty dozen." This was the best job I could've asked for. I would be working with eleven other girls cleaning the head after showers both in the morning and the evening. What made this job the best? The women's bathroom was the one place that the male drill instructors could not enter unless they announced themselves. The showers stood in the corner, which meant I could easily stay out of sight and out of mind. Boy, was I right. When two weeks passed, as the division stood at attention ready to go outside to practice, the BM1 looked at her roster.

"Do we have a Taylor in this group?"

The chief and OS1 both shrugged their shoulders.

"Never seen her in our division."

Darn, I thought to myself. *Now they'll know my name. I won't be able to hide out any longer.* Looking straight ahead, I shouted, "Ma'am, yes, ma'am." All three drill instructors looked at me.

"Damn, Taylor, have you been here the whole time?"

I answered again. "Ma'am, yes, ma'am."

BM1 stepped toward me and squinted her eyes.

"Taylor, were you trying to stay hidden?"

"Ma'am, yes, ma'am," I answered.

I could tell that she wanted to start laughing, but she forced the smile from her face and became serious. We were about to go flag marching. I knew that they would be watching me now, especially since they knew I'd been trying to hide.

After we finished practicing flag marching, which I enjoyed, it was time for my favorite part of the day: chow. Whether it was breakfast, lunch, or dinner, chow was my favorite. The food was delicious, plus chow created a chance to sit down and relax. We couldn't talk to anyone, but I didn't care.

Because I'm short, I always stood third in line. This worked to my benefit. It gave me extra time to eat and relax. Once the last person in our division sat down to eat, we had fifteen minutes before leaving the chow hall. The cooks were civilian and were really nice. Sometimes they would bring around a new recipe for us to try. Of course, we couldn't answer them, but if we raised our hands, they would serve us a bowl of their new dish.

Once we got back to the barracks, it was time for the drill instructors to give us intensive training (IT). Really, IT provided an opportunity for them to torture us. Actually, I didn't mind. IT gave us a chance to work off what we'd eaten that night. Besides, the exercises weren't that bad for those who came to boot camp in pretty good shape. IT sessions usually lasted about an hour, but then they were over. Afterward, they usually made us clean the barracks and shine our shoes before lights-out. We had to turn one sock inside out and then put it over our hands. On our hands and knees, we crawled around on the floor looking for ghost turds. Ghost turds are little balls of fuzz otherwise referred to as dust bunnies. It was really gross. Not only did we pick up dirt and fuzz from the floor, far too often we picked up balls of hair, which had to be picked off by hand and thrown in the trash.

That night after showers, the drill instructors told us that we would be changing racks and rack buddies. I was told to move from my rack by the drill instructor's office to the corner rack. I felt so excited. That rack made the easiest hideout. The drill instructors couldn't easily see back there. My new rack partner was a girl by the name of Shrieder. I'd spoken to her a couple of times. We got along really well. She also had a family and kids. She showed me pictures of her two sons and her husband. I showed her my pictures and shared letters I received from my daughter, Aria, and my husband, John.

The next morning, we'd be taking our physical readiness test (PRT), which we had to pass in order to complete boot camp. Before the test, the Catholic chaplain came into the barracks to talk to us. He mentioned that he needed singers and musicians to play in church. Practice would take place on Friday afternoon and we were free to leave the barracks in order to attend. We would also get out of the barracks on Sunday morning for service. Always thinking ahead, I raised my hand and said, "I play the violin."

The chaplain looked at me and smiled. "I would love to have you," he said. "I happen to have a couple of violins. You can borrow one. I'm learning to play."

Looking at Shrieder, I told her that she should let the chaplain know that she sang. She looked at me with a strange expression on her face. "I don't sing."

I whispered, "You do now. Don't you want to get out of here?"

Smiling, she raised her hand and told the chaplain, "I sing."

From that day on, we both went to practice together on Fridays and then to mass on Sundays. It was great. I played the violin and she sang in the choir.

As weeks passed, I got used to being at boot camp. The only thing I wasn't looking forward to was getting my Pap smear done at medical. I had a hard time sleeping the night before. It's an exam I just don't like. Who really does? An unfamiliar person using strange tools goes into something private. The day of the Pap, I wanted it over with. As they finished the exam, I was told to wait outside for my results. I waited for hours, desperately wanting to be cleared to go back to the barracks. When I was finally called into the doctor's office, I was told to take a seat. The doctor told me she'd put me on medical hold. I became scared. Why was she putting me on medical hold? What was wrong with me? She told me I would need another exam to check my cervix. I couldn't swallow. My stomach began to hurt and I felt short of breath.

Looking at me with no compassion, the doctor blurted, "Taylor, we found cancer cells and we need to double-check before you're passed through medical."

Can you imagine a person blurting the word cancer so easily? It seemed as if the word *cancer* meant nothing to her. Trying not to cry, I agreed to the exam.

I was told that I needed to come into medical the next day. How could I sleep that night? My first thoughts were of my daughter, Aria. If I had cancer and something happened to me, what would her life be like?

The next day, I went back for the cervix exam. As I lay down on the table, I couldn't see a thing. A sheet hid the lower half of my body. As my legs were placed in the stirrups, I felt an instrument being inserted inside me. Tears began to collect on the inner corner of my eyes and I slowly gripped the table tighter and tighter. Just as my body began to tense, a sharp and intense pain struck inside me. I had never experienced anything like it. I was kept on the exam table for about fifteen minutes. What was taking so long? Just after I felt another intense pain, my whole lower abdomen began to cramp. It felt as though someone slashed the inside of my cervix. As the doctor removed the instrument, she said, "You're done. You can get dressed and go back to your barracks." The door opened and a few people stepped outside the room. I didn't know what they'd done. I didn't know why the procedure had taken so long or why so many people had been in the room. I felt scared because I'd been unable to see what they were doing. All I knew was that it hurt.

As I took my legs down from the stirrups, I felt as though someone had torn me from the inside. Slowly peeling myself off the table, I noticed blood on the inside of my thighs. The color red had never looked so intense, staining the whitest part of my legs. Pulling on my white underwear, I could already see the blood begin to stain the material. Once dressed, I placed my green belt and canteen back on my waist. I was told I didn't need a special medical chit or note. Instead, I was told to run back to the barracks, which was a good three miles. The sun shone hot upon my face. The more I tried to run, the more my abdomen cramped.

My run became more of a shuffle because of the pain. I couldn't even pick up my feet. Entering my barracks, I reported to the drill instructor's office. The only drill instructor there was BM1. As she stood from her chair, she approached me with care and compassion.

"Taylor, what did they say and how did it go?"

I couldn't hold my composure. Tears welled in my eyes and my cheeks became hot. I blurted out, stuttering, "They.... they clipped me from the inside and said they think it's cancer. They've put me on hold. It…It hurt." Wiping my eyes, I continued. "I'm still bleeding and have really bad cramps."

I was surprised by BM1's concern. She gave me a hug, told me to calm myself, and then told me to sit so that she could talk to me. As she sat in the chair facing me, she looked straight at me and said, "I know what you are going through. They did the same thing to me when I came here as a drill instructor. I was OK and you will be OK."

Just then, OS1 came in and asked BM1 if she was ready to go. The other recruits were lined up to go marching. BM1 asked again if I was OK to go. I told her I would be fine.

As I walked out the door to get into formation, the chief yelled, "Taylor, you're late. Get in line." BM1 ran over and whispered something to the chief and to OS1. The chief's face turned from anger to concern. All three drill instructors looked at me as the chief yelled, "Taylor, go to the back of the line and don't march. Just walk behind everyone." That was the first time I ever saw a drill instructor show compassion. After that day, I continued with boot camp as though nothing had ever happened. I knew that I was still on medical hold, but I would have to wait and see what they said.

Only a few more weeks remained. I'd completed firefighting training, which was my favorite, and I'd gone through the gas chamber. Boy, I could sure use going through that chamber more often. Yes, it burned my face, eyes, throat, but with all of my sinus problems, for the first time in my life I could really breathe through my nose. It was as if I'd been in the movie "Ghostbusters" and had just gotten slimed.

With so little time left in boot camp, the chief called over to medical to ask about my status. They told him I remained on medical hold. While sitting on the floor and polishing my boot, the chief came by and told me to go to medical. I felt so scared. I didn't know what they were going to say and I was not prepared to hear bad news. Walking into the office, I took a seat and was told that someone would be right with me. Two hours later, while I was still sitting in the waiting room, OS1 entered. He sat down next to me and asked, "Taylor, are you still waiting to be seen?"

"Yes, sir," I answered. "I've been here for two hours."

OS1 looked disgusted and walked up to the medical counters. He was there for a good while. When he returned, he said I would be going in soon and that I never should have waited that long. Just before he left, OS1 turned around and said, "Taylor, it will be OK. Let me know what happens as soon as you get out of here."

I told him I would let him know. Just as he walked out, I was called in to see the doctor. I was asked to sit in the same seat where I'd received bad news before. This time, the doctor told me I was medically clear and could leave. Was that it? Well, I guess I didn't have cancer. I was completely baffled. She had scared me to no end before and now she acted as though it was nothing. How could she do this to a person? I stood up and left the medical offices in disbelief. Entering my barracks, I walked up to OS1.

"Sir, I am medically cleared. Everything was fine, I guess."

"Good," he said half-smiling. "I'm glad you're OK. Now," he screamed into my face, "get back to shining your boots!" At that moment, I felt thrilled to hear the drill instructor scream at me. Everything had returned to normal.

Graduation day came. I would no longer be a recruit. Instead, I had become a navy sailor. As I stood in the women's head of division 933 barracks, I straightened my combination cap feeling both excited and nervous. I had been waiting for this day. I would officially graduate from boot camp. It seemed so unbelievable. I had never thought I could put myself though such a mentally and physically exhausting atmosphere. As the oldest female in my division — thirty years old to be exact — I had a lot to prove. My friend Shrieder stood next to me having trouble creating the slipknot in her neckerchief.

"I can't believe we made it, Taylor. Are you excited to see your daughter and the rest of your family?"

I leaned over to finish tying her neckerchief.

"Yes, very," I said. "I never thought this day would come. The only problem is it will be hard not to go back with my family after graduation. I am excited to see Aria. My husband's bringing her and my parents are coming, too. We still have our schools after this, though."

Shrieder bent down to check the laces on her shoes. "I wish we were going to A school together," she said. "I'll be in Mississippi and you'll be here in Great Lakes."

"We'll always stay in touch," I told her and we gave each other a hug.

"Are you guys ready?" interrupted our friend, Grant. "It's time."

Graduation flew by. After putting away my flag and checking out with the drill instructors, I was able to spend the rest of the day with my family. Though that meant simply going to get Steak 'n Shake, it was nice to have a restful day without any yelling. I knew that I would have to stay for A school, but I couldn't keep my emotions from overpowering me. More than anything, I wanted to go home with my family to San Diego. I always had my daughter on my mind, wondering what she was doing and what I was missing. I tried to remember that she was my motivation. She was my reason to keep going.

I graduated from OS class A school as one of the top students. Going to night school on my own during the week, I graduated a couple of months early. Though the classes were a lot of hard work, I knew that becoming an OS was what I wanted. I wanted to learn a technical skill. I wanted to work with radars doing surveillance in a combat environment. A school was a lot different than boot camp. I actually enjoyed boot camp more because I got used to the discipline. A school had rules to follow, but it was very laid back. Although Shrieder was in Mississippi, Grant, who was going to BM school, was in my barracks. We spent almost all of our weekends together. We had lunch and dinner together every day. I have to say that I made a lot of friends in A school, but I was still ready to go home.

At the end of September, I knew that I would still have to wait at the barracks on hold to receive orders. Because I graduated early and had been a good student, the command master chief (CMC) of the school requested that I come work in his office during the week. I couldn't have been more excited. Rather than staying at the barracks all day cleaning, I went to the school to help with filing and paperwork. I had a great time working with the CMC and the civilians in his office up to the middle of October. After a good day's work, I walked into the barracks when the first class petty officer on duty stopped me.

"Taylor, I've got something for you. You got your orders. Looks like you'll be leaving us. You'll be going to the USS Russiantown, which is stationed in San Diego. Looks like they want you there as soon as possible before they leave on a six-month deployment."

I thought to myself, *Six-month deployment...*

I tried to keep a serious expression on my face, but the excitement took over. I was going home and that was all I could think of at the moment. For the time being, I didn't have time to think about leaving for six months. I grabbed my orders, took a deep breath, and walked up to my room. I couldn't move fast enough to find my phone to call home and let them know that I was coming. That night, I lay in bed and thought about what it would be like once I got home. What would the future hold? What would my new command be like?

CHAPTER TWO

The Fire

In October of 2007, I made it home from A school. It was a couple of weeks before Halloween and I was happy to be able to take Aria trick-or-treating. I hadn't been home but a week when OS1 Green called from the USS Russiantown. She wanted to know if I could cut my vacation by a week to come to the ship early and learn my way around before leaving on deployment. I really didn't want to, but I didn't want to leave a bad impression. I told her I would be there on Monday. The Friday night before, my family and I sat around watching TV. A series of fires had been set around California.

My father stayed focused on the TV. "We are going to need to watch the Valley Center fire," he said. "It looks like it's headed toward our house. We might want to start packing up some of the cars just in case."

My first instinct was fear and a feeling that I'd better start packing.

"I don't think it's that close," responded John. "We still have time."

I didn't care what he had to say. I planned to start packing some of our things. After a few hours, fire trucks and police entered our gated community as the fire had come up over the hill. After my mom, grandma, Aria, and I had packed the cars, we were the first to take off to head to my aunt and uncle's house. My father and John stayed behind to hose down the house and the yard. By the time they finished watering, the ash from the fire was coming down thick. The fire was close. The cops came around and told them to evacuate immediately. Eventually, they made it to my aunt and uncle's house, where my cousin, his wife, and their four kids also lived. We weren't quite sure where we would sleep, but it was a safe place. To drive anywhere from Escondido would be too difficult. Major fires burned in San Diego and parts of the I-15 freeway had been closed. Fires burned north of San Diego, too, along State Route 78 in San Marcos. The fires had come full circle.

Staying with my aunt and uncle was fun. My husband, Aria, and I slept on the floor. My grandma slept on the recliner and my parents slept on the couch. We sat around the TV most of the day deciding what to eat for breakfast, lunch, and dinner, and then someone would go get the food for our feast. Then we'd continue to watch the fire on the news.

By Monday, the fires burned even hotter and had gained ground. I tried to figure out how to get to my first day of work on the ship. I decided to call OS1 Green to let her know that I might be late.

"That's fine," she said. "Thank you for letting me know. Get here when you can."

On Monday morning, I drove down to the ship with my car stacked to the top. John, on the other hand, an active duty marine, was told not to come in due to the fires. Driving down to the ship was so scary. I couldn't take I-15, so I crossed over the 78 to Oceanside and then took the 5 freeway down. All I could hear was the sound of sirens. The traffic was horrible. Most of the cars were stacked with items up to the very top. Others must have evacuated also. I didn't dare roll down my car windows. The air seemed thick with ash; the sky showed very little hint of blue. A dark, gray cloud hovered, which from a distance showed a red tint. A couple of hours later, I reported to the USS Russiantown. The ship looked huge standing apart from the other navy ships. Green met me at the quarterdeck. The quarterdeck is where one salutes the officer of the deck (OOD) or a senior enlisted on duty in order to come aboard a ship. Green told me she would take me to my rack, or the bed where I would be sleeping, first. They call the beds coffin racks because the spaces are so tight. Under the bed is a compartment for storing things like sanitary items, socks, underwear, or anything small enough to fit into the space.

"We have muster every morning on the 06 level at 0800. Once I show you your rack, I'll take you to the combat information center or (CIC) room. Most everyone is there."

As we entered women's berthing, she told me my rack would be on top. I thought to myself, *How the heck am I going to get up to the top rack? I'm going to need a ladder.* I followed Green down the passageway or p-way toward the aft of the ship where she opened a cipher-locked door and told me to step inside. I noticed three groups of radars on my left and one radar on its own in a corner. It took a moment for my eyes to adjust to the dark. I had never felt so uncomfortable in my life. As I looked around the room, I realized that everyone was staring at me. Green introduced me.

"This is OS3 Taylor. She's checking in today and I'm showing her around."

A young girl with black hair pulled into a perfect bun turned away from the radar. Green pointed to her.

"This is OS3 Vale."

Green announced that the girl next to Vale would be showing me around the ship and training me while I was on deployment. She seemed very nice.

"Hi," she said. "My name is Smith."

Behind her sat two other girls. One looked as though she might be Indian. Her features were very unique. She had very tan skin and black hair. She introduced herself as Flannery. Her friend, who was very small and thin, was Nicolette. Both girls looked me up and down, making me feel even more uncomfortable than I already felt. I turned my attention to the next person, a second class. He looked goofy with his blond, spiky hair and a smirk on his face. As soon as he opened his mouth, I could tell he must be the jokester of the group.

"So, do you find me good looking?" he asked and then started laughing.

I didn't know what to say, so I just looked at him and laughed a nervous laugh.

"I'm Kowlesky," he said.

Standing next to him and staring down at me was the biggest man I have ever seen in my life. He shook my hand.

"Hi, I'm Chief Weinerbangher," he said. "They also call me OSC, Chief of Operation Specialists, or just Chief. I heard you had to evacuate because of the fires. What are you doing here? You shouldn't have come in."

I looked at him surprised and said sheepishly, "I didn't know not to come in. I was told to report today."

He glared at me then proceeded. "Who told you that? Do you have all your things in your car?"

"OS1 Green told me to come in. I have everything in my car from when my family and I evacuated. It's here on base," I answered.

"Where are you staying?"

"My family and I are staying in Escondido with my aunt and uncle," I replied.

"Go home," he said assertively. "Call every day to check in, but don't come back until you're back in your home and your family is safe."

I agreed, told him that it was nice meeting him, and then walked out of CIC. Smith stood behind me. She followed me to the berthing area.

"So," she said, "what do you think so far? Are you ready to go on deployment?"

"No, not really," I said.

As she raised her coffin rack, I realized that she slept in the rack under my bed. I asked her, "How do I get up into my bed?"

She laughed and said, "Here, I'll show you."

She faced the rack, put her left foot on the bottom rack, and then lifted her right foot placing it on the middle rack. With a slight push, she slid right into my rack.

"It just takes practice," she said.

The berthing door opened and a girl with red hair and freckles walked in. She looked at me and said in a southern accent, "You must be new. My name is McGraw."

As she spoke, I couldn't help but smell the stench of cigarettes on her breath. She also had very yellow teeth. Smith spoke up. She told McGraw that I was new and that my name was Taylor. McGraw shook my hand and then walked off to get back to work.

"McGraw's rack is across the way on the bottom," Smith informed me. "She's hard to get along with. She has a temper and has to fight with everyone. She also stinks and her rack stinks."

"Thanks for the info. Did I meet all of the OSs on the ship in the CIC?" I asked.

"No," Smith responded. "There are more, but some people are off today."

I gathered my things and told Smith I would see her later. Walking off the ship, I still felt like I was dreaming. I asked myself, *What in the world are you doing? Are you crazy?* Everything seemed surreal. At least I was off the ship and heading to my aunt and uncle's house. It took me two hours before I made it back as traffic had grown worse. I could see the fire in San Marcos from the 78 freeway. Once I made it to the house, I noticed an extra car in the driveway. Friends of my aunt and uncle who had also evacuated had come to stay with them. In total, sixteen people were staying in their one-story, three-bedroom house.

As each day passed, we received little to no information about our house. There was no information on the news about our area. My mother and I tried to drive down to look at the house, but the National Guard had blocked off the road. My mother and I asked what was happening and if the houses were alright, but they didn't have any information.

Five days went by before we were allowed to return to our house. The whole community was covered in ash. The fire had come up to our backyard. In order to get to the fire in a hurry, the fire department broke down the back fence between the neighbor's house and ours. Holes had burned all over the cushions of the patio furniture also. That night, we all felt relieved that the fires were out. We also felt so thankful that the firemen had been able to save our house. I was glad that the fires were in control now and that I would be able to celebrate Halloween with Aria before leaving on deployment. We almost thought we wouldn't be able to celebrate the holiday because of the fires.

On Halloween, Aria came up to me and asked, "Mommy, what am I going to be for Halloween? I don't have a costume and you said you were going to get me one."

"Oh my gosh, Aria, I forgot. With everything going on, I didn't think about it."

In a panic, I drove with my mom to the store to see what costumes I could find. Everything was sold out. The only thing I could find was caution tape. What was I going to do with that? Then, an idea came to mind. I looked down the next aisle over and saw that Christmas decorations were already out. A zombie elf. Why not? I knew I was running out of time to put something together. When I got home, Aria looked at me like I was crazy. I dressed her in two different knee-high socks, a pair of jean shorts, suspenders, and a crazy top. I wrapped her whole body with the caution tape, put zombie-like makeup on her face, and finished the look with a Santa hat. She stood in front of the mirror, quietly looking at herself. I apologized again for forgetting about her costume. As my mom and I stood staring at Aria, we couldn't help but laugh.

"I bet no one will have a costume like you," I told her.

I don't think she bought what I had to say, but it wasn't really about the costume. She soon forgot, overcome with excitement to go from house to house to get candy.

CHAPTER THREE

Sea and Anchor

Halloween came and went. Before I knew it, it was November 4, the day I would be leaving for a six-month deployment. Though I felt too old to cry, I couldn't keep away the tears. I felt as though my heart had dropped into my stomach and I could no longer swallow given the rock in my throat. My eyes were swollen from crying and I wondered if I'd made the wrong decision in joining the navy. That morning, John drove me to the ship. Aria was also in the car and came to see me sail off. My parents and grandma followed behind. As we parked in front of the ship, I froze. I didn't want to get out of the car. I knew there was no backing out now and I had to show Aria that I was strong. I grabbed my seabag from the car and hugged my family goodbye. I didn't hesitate. I knew the best way would be for me to leave quickly. As I walked down the pier, I wanted to cry again, but I knew that I couldn't. I couldn't turn around and look at them because I knew I would get emotional. Walking tall with my eyes straight ahead, I entered the ship and walked straight to the berthing area.

"Hey, as soon as you're ready, we need to get to CIC," Smith exclaimed putting snacks into her coffin rack. "They're going to have muster there to tell us where we're supposed to go for sea and anchor detail. Come on. You'll also get to meet the rest of the OSs."

I followed her down the p-way as other sailors hurried about getting ready to set sail. The p-ways were considered the hallways of the ship. I entered CIC and noticed that it was crowded with people I'd never met. Right away, Green started introducing me to the other OS sailors. I focused my attention on a small, Hispanic guy who was smiling. He appeared to be very friendly. As I shook his hand, I noticed the name Gomez on his overalls. He must have been in for a while because he was a second class. Next to him stood a very tall, serious-looking guy with sand-colored hair who appeared older than the rest of the OSs. He seemed familiar to me, though I couldn't quite make out why at first. Could he be a famous actor? Then, it came to me. He looked like the actor and comedian Will Ferrell, although he did not appear to have a sense of humor. Green introduced us. She told me his name was Martel. In the corner, the last of the OSs were preparing the digital dead reckoning tracer (DDRT) for sea and anchor detail. I could see some of the OSs placing white drawing paper over the DDRT surface and making sure the pencils were sharpened. Green leaned over and told me that the girl's name was Weissman and the guy's name was Cameron. Weissman seemed nice but very focused. She was very tall and dark in color, as was Cameron. As I looked at him, I noticed that he was smiling at me.

"Hey," he said, trying to sound like Rico Suave. "What's up?"

"Hi," I said quietly.

Cameron just kept staring, acting like he thought he was the sexiest man on earth.

Oh brother, I thought. *Is this what I'm going to have to deal with for six months?*

As I stood looking around the room, I felt very uncomfortable. I didn't know what to do and I didn't know what to expect. I also found it weird that I was on a ship and I hadn't met the commanding officer (CO) or the executive officer (XO) yet. I knew the CO was CDR Vermont and the XO was LCDR Dennis. The ranking for officers in the navy is Ensign (ENS) O-1, Lieutenant Junior Grade (LTJG) O-2, Lieutenant (LT) O-3, Lieutenant Commander (LCDR) O-4, Commander (CDR) O-5, Captain (CAPT) O-6, and at the top is various ranks of Admiral. I imagined how busy they must have been, getting the personnel and the ship ready to set sail. Just as I thought I had met everyone otherwise, a tall, thin man with red hair walked in. He was an OS and wore the chevrons of a second class. I saw him look over at me as he walked across the room. As Green was busy staging everyone for sea and anchor detail, I looked at his name tag, which said Campbell.

Everyone in the room remained focused on their jobs. Within the CIC, fire controlmen (FC) and cryptologic technicians (CT) were at work as well. Green told me that since I was new, I would be going to the flight deck for sea and anchor detail. She told Smith to go with me.

"We'll be standing at parade rest as the ship sails off," said Smith. "We'll be standing there for a while."

Shortly thereafter, I heard a horn go off on ship. Over the intercom, someone said, "Prepare for sea and anchor detail."

I followed Smith and then stood at the edge of the ship on the flight deck. I felt a cool breeze on my face. As I looked into the distance to my right, I could see my family waving and watching me sail away. Although they knew that I couldn't wave back, they knew that I saw them. Slowly and smoothly, the ship pulled away from the dock. I watched as my family became smaller and smaller. It felt like flying on a plane and looking out the window as everything becomes miniature. Within minutes, my family disappeared, replaced with the buildings of San Diego and the Coronado Bridge directly above. I thought to myself, *Am I ready for this?*

CHAPTER FOUR

Training

When the whistle blew ending sea and anchor detail, I followed Smith back to CIC. Green was already busy deciding who would be on each watch schedule. We all worked twelve hours on and then took twelve hours off. Since I was new, Smith would sit with me and train me for at least two weeks. Green told me that I would be on the second watch, which would come on at 1700. She told me I was free to do what I wanted until then. Green suggested that we all get some sleep. Walking out of CIC, I made a mental note that the rest of my watch team consisted of OS1 Weissman, OS2 Gomez, OSSN Flannery, OSSN Nicolette, and OS2 Campbell. OS2 was close to making OS1 but it appeared that he wasn't going to re-enlist in the Navy. I had heard him mention to someone that he had less than a year left in the Navy and was going to get out.

Right away, everyone rushed over to the OS office which was the Battle Force Tactical Training room (BFFT). BFFT contained computers for accessing e-mail and the Internet. I stepped outside for a breath of fresh air on the 06 level. As I stood along the railing, I looked at the surrounding ocean. As the water splashed up on the side of the ship, white foam formed, skimming across the blue. The air felt fresh across my face. This was a moment for me to be by myself and to gather my thoughts. I thought about home, my family, and how lonely I felt. At once, I felt a presence at my side. Looking up, I saw OSC. He smelled of smoke. He must have come from the smoke deck on the ship where a crowd of sailors gathered.

"Everything OK?" he asked.

"Yes," I answered. "I just came out for some fresh air. I was thinking about my family and feeling homesick."

"That's understandable. It will get better," he said in a positive voice. "You have a daughter, right?"

I nodded.

"I have a son who's ten years old. How old is your daughter?"

Pausing a moment, I answered, "She's nine."

"We'll be home before you know it. If there's anything I can do for you or if you need anyone to talk to, let me know."

I smiled at him as he walked down the stairs looking back at me a few times.

As I was about to go back inside the ship, I saw McGraw of the smoke deck. She called me over. I entered the dark cloud of smoke and noticed that a couple of the marines looked familiar. Due to the fact that I'm a nosey person, I asked what company they were with and if they knew my husband, Staff Sergeant Taylor. My assumptions were correct. They did know him and used to work with him. Sadly, none of them liked him. As it turned out, according to them, he had poor leadership skills and only thought of himself. I must admit that I wasn't surprised to hear them say that. After all, I'd been married to him for eleven years. I knew that he took care of himself and forgot the needs of others. I guess there were a lot of people that didn't like him. I was married to the man and I could barely stand him.

After talking to them for a few moments, I couldn't handle the smoke any longer. I went down to berthing to take a nap. As I walked inside, I noticed that Smith was already asleep. I quietly put on my sweats and crawled up into my rack. Before shutting my eyes, I said a prayer to God to help me get through deployment. I asked him to take care of my family and to let me have a good first watch.

Seven hours later, I woke to my alarm. I got dressed and went down to the mess decks to get some dinner before watch. Standing in line, I again felt uncomfortable. There were so many people that I didn't know staring at me because I was new. At the front of the line, Smith came down and asked if she could eat with me. Naturally, I said yes. She was really nice and I didn't want to eat alone. I let her cut in line. The food didn't look very appetizing, but I felt hungry. I put mashed potatoes on my plate with a piece of meat loaf. Looking down the line, I noticed a salad bar. Grabbing the tongs, I leaned forward and grabbed some lettuce. Just as I was about to put it on my plate, I saw something brown dangling. It was a giant cockroach. Completely disgusted, I put the lettuce back in the bowl. The guy behind me looked grossed out as well and yelled to the cooks that there was a cockroach on the salad bar. I looked over at the shredded cheddar cheese and saw a baby cockroach come running out. Needless to say, I lost my appetite completely. Smith and I found a place to sit, put down our trays, and began talking about the different people on the ship and what watch would be like. I was going to have to learn a lot of different things. In the middle of our conversation, I heard someone say my name and sit down next to me.

"Taylor, I haven't seen you on the ship," said a tall guy with sandy-brown hair and glasses. "How's it going?" It was a friend of mine from A school, Quartermaster (QMSN) Richards. We were in the same barracks. Next to him sat another friend from school, QMSN Montgomery, who was Richards' roommate at the barracks in A school.

"Hey," I said. "What are you guys doing? I am so glad to see you guys." I pointed at Smith, introducing her.

"Hello," said Montgomery. "This is QMSN Schuemaker."

"Hi," I responded. He was a very tall and thin guy with a large and noticeable nose. He wasn't bad-looking, but his nose was simply the most noticeable thing about him. "When we get to some of the ports, we should hang out together."

"That would be cool," Richards said.

As Smith stood up and motioned for me to follow, I knew it was time to go on watch.

"I have to go on watch, but have any of you seen Davis?" I asked. "I thought he was going to the Russiantown? I haven't seen him since A school."

Richards nodded and said that they had seen him. I told him to say hi to him for me if he sees him. On that note, I took off walking to CIC.

As Smith and I entered CIC, Campbell told us that we would start on the radar together to relieve Vale. Campbell would be the OS in charge of our watch. He wasn't part of the rotation; his job was to make sure that the lower-ranking personnel performed their jobs correctly. As Vale got off the seat and took the sound-powered telephones from her head, Smith slid into the corner spot in front of the radar and put on the headset. A sound-powered telephone allows users to talk to eachother on different areas of the ship without using a handset. It does not use external power. A sound-powered phone circuit can have two or more stations on the same circuit. Therefore, the circuit is live and a user does not have to dial into another station. They can just being speaking to one another.

Smith told me to pull up a chair behind her while she explained how to track and label the contacts on the radar. As Nicolette entered CIC, Campbell told her to go up to the bridge and relieve McGraw on the radar. Nicolette made an unhappy face, and then left CIC to go up to the bridge. Flannery relieved Cameron on the DDRT. I really didn't like the fact that she was on our watch team. She seemed unfriendly and full of herself. I could see Weissman sitting quietly at a radar in the back of the room. Gomez was on the front air radar. He always smiled at me and asked how I was doing, offering to help me in any way that he could. Since we were short a person to run the charts until I received proper training, Campbell took on the job of plotting where the ship was headed.

My first day on the job, everything seemed confusing. I didn't know how I'd be able to learn everything. As the night progressed and Smith and I rotated between CIC and the bridge, I began to feel like I was catching on. Of course, I would need a lot more practice. Around 0200, Smith and I were on the DDRT. OSC was on one of the front radars. Smith had told me that OSC always had watch at night. She said that his job was the tactical action officer (TAO). I heard everyone laughing quietly, so I turned around and saw OSC sound asleep in his chair. He'd warned us that there would be no sleeping on the job. It seemed there was a double standard for him. Campbell told me that he usually slept while he worked.

As we all laughed, I noticed that Smith wasn't laughing. She looked frustrated.

"Is something wrong?" I asked her.

"They're saying things about me over the phones," she answered.

"Who?" I asked. "What are they saying?"

"They're saying that I smell. They're asking me why I'm so fat and ugly." Smith sounded as if she were about to cry.

"What?" I couldn't believe what I was hearing. "Why would they be saying anything? Your not those things they are saying at all. We just left for deployment and they are already starting a fight?"

As she placed the phones over my ears, I could hear Nicolette and Flannery talking about Smith with one of the BMs on watch. They said that she didn't shower and smelled bad. I didn't say a word, but just listened. Finally, I gave the phones back to Smith. I felt badly for her. They continued to taunt her all morning until we got off watch.

The twelve hours of watch went by slowly. By the time I got off, I went down and got a quick bite for breakfast with Smith. I spoke with her about what had happened and tried to find out why they didn't like her. Smith didn't know herself. I didn't know what to say or how to help her. I thought that the best thing I could do was to be her friend. Leaving the mess decks, we both went up to bed.

I set my alarm making sure to give myself extra time to go down to the gym before dinner and then back on watch again. After an early rise and a work-out, I felt very refreshed. I took a shower and then planned to get a bite to eat and go outside on the 06 level to enjoy the breeze. This was my chance to get away from everyone and to think. As I went across the smoke deck, I saw OSC looking at me. He sat on a wooden bench smoking a cigarette. Feeling him stare at me, I continued to walk up the stairs to the 07 level. There were look-out binoculars attached to the ship through which I could see far out into the ocean. The sun had started to set and the sky appeared bright orange and yellow. The sky's reflection made the water look as though someone had set it ablaze. It looked beautiful and so relaxing. As I looked up, I felt as though someone was standing behind me. I could tell it was someone much bigger than me since the shadow engulfed my own. It was OSC.

"What are you doing up here?" he said staring at me.

"I was looking out into the water and watching the sun set before I go on watch."

He looked me up and down, and then continued. "You know, it can get lonely being out to sea." He slowly walked toward me. Instead of having his sleeves down, he had them rolled up tight against his fat, white arms. I could feel the hair around his wrist lightly touch my hand.

"Yes, it can," I said.

Looking at me eye-to-eye, he spoke quietly. "Well, I guess I'll see you in watch." Then he turned and walked away.

That was weird, I thought to myself. It felt as though he'd been staring at my body, studying it. *After the talk he'd given me about sexual harassment when I got on the ship, he couldn't possibly be coming on to me.* I wondered if it was me, if I was just being paranoid.

Just after OSC left, three marines came up to the look-out area.

"How's it going?" one asked.

"Good," I said.

Another of them came over to me. He was shorter than the other marines. He had blond hair and a wide smile that caused creases on his face around his mouth. I could tell from the insignia on his uniform that he was a staff sergeant.

"So, Taylor, what's your first name?" he asked as he shook my hand.

"My name is Lisa," I answered.

"My name is Staff Sergeant (SSgt) Andy Williams. Why are you up here by yourself?"

Why did everyone want to know why I was by myself? I felt like I couldn't get any quiet time alone.

I answered abruptly. "Just thinking."

He looked at me, smiled, and then looked out to the ocean.

"I'm gonna go on watch," I said. "It was nice meeting you." I left to go downstairs to watch and back to training with Smith.

A couple of weeks passed and did so faster than I could've possibly imagined. The time came for me to enter the watch cycle myself. Almost immediately after I placed the phones on my ears, I heard Flannery talking about Smith and saying that she smelled. Smith was pretty fired up and began shooting back her own comments at Flannery and Nicolette. At one point, Campbell tried to stop the fighting, but it didn't stop. I never found out what started the fight between them. I never asked. I wondered if they even knew why they hated each other so much. Looking around the room, I saw Campbell look over to the TAO watch station.

"Hey, someone needs to go and wake up Chief," Campbell said.

Just then, Kowlesky walked into CIC.

"Kowlesky," Campbell said. "Go wake up Chief."

Kowlesky shook his head. "You go wake him up. He scares me. He barely fits in his rack then he sleeps in his tighty-whities with his big, hairy belly sticking out. Plus, he turns around and makes snorting noises while he's trying to take off his oxygen mask."

Watching Kowlesky imitate the chief was so funny. It was if he was imitating Frankenstein's monster getting out of bed in the morning. Then I thought to myself, *Did he say oxygen mask? I didn't know the navy allowed a sailor to go on deployment with an oxygen mask.*

"Just go," Campbell told him.

A few moments later, Kowlesky came running into CIC gagging and holding his noise.

"I am never doing that again," he said. "Ugh! I've been scarred for life!" He ran around CIC, acting as though he was about to throw up. A couple of times he even started dry-heaving. Whether or not he was acting, I didn't know. Campbell started laughing and asked Kowlesky what happened.

Between gags, Kowlesky said, "I walked in to wake up Chief and he was sleeping on top of the sheets in his tighty-whities. He was on his side so that his butt was facing me. When I poked him to wake him up, he let out the loudest fart ever. I almost passed out. It smelled like something crawled up his butt and died. Then he turned around with his mask on, took it off, and then yawned. His breath smelled like someone took a crap in his mouth."

No one could resist laughing at that point. We were all cracking up. This was the first time I'd seen Campbell laugh so hard that tears came out of his eyes. Watching all of us laugh at him, Kowlesky just shook his head and walked out of CIC. Soon after Kowlesky left, OSC walked in looking disheveled. He quietly went to his seat as TAO and didn't say much all night.

Once 1200 came around, it was time for mid-rats. Mid-rats (short for midnight rations) is when all the yummy food from dinner is reheated and served again. When I say yummy, I mean that sarcastically. Eating dog food out of a can would taste better than anything that cockroach-infested ship could serve. Smith and I took our break together. Instead of going down to the mess decks, Smith told me that her parents had sent her some snacks that she would share with me. As we walked up to her rack to open it, she stopped and looked closely at the top. Because it was so dark in the berthing, it was hard to see. Plus, the red light made it more difficult to adjust one's eyes.

"What is that?" she asked.

Smith turned on her light and we looked down to discover blood smeared all over her white, satin pillow. It appeared as though a female had taken a used menstrual pad and smeared it everywhere. In a fit of anger, Smith stormed out of berthing and went straight to CIC to show Campbell. I followed behind. Smith had a hunch that Flannery and Nicolette had something to do with it. Although I didn't know them very well, I had a feeling that Smith was right.

"Flannery and Nicolette did this. I know they did." Smith sounded irritated. Her eyes pierced through Nicolette who was on the radar in the corner. If Smith could have jumped over and choked Nicolette with her bare hands, she would have. I didn't blame her.

Chief stood up from his chair and asked what was going on.

"Flannery and Nicolette smeared blood all over my pillow. I know it was them. They've been giving me a hard time since leaving on deployment. Other people have heard them calling me names on the phones. I want them written up and taken to captain's mast."

Chief walked out with Smith to calm her down. Campbell told me to get back on my station. After about an hour, they both came back in. The next thing I knew, Chief called Flannery out to talk. He told Nicolette that he would talk to her after watch.

The rest of watch was silent. No one talked except when surface or air contact was nearby. That night while on watch on the bridge radar, I met QM3 Edwin. She was African American. She was slim built and fairly attractive but liked to pick fights with everyone. She acted as though she was always completely miserable. Edwin was slender and not bad looking, but her disposition made her ugly. Because I was new, I think she thought that she could intimidate me. Since the OSs and QMs worked together on the ship for navigation purposes, I knew I would have a run-in with her sooner or later. As she came over to my area to grab a rag, Edwin used her elbow to move me out of the way. She didn't bother to say excuse me.

Since it was dark, Edwin couldn't see the nasty look on my face. I turned around and said, "Excuse you."

Walking back with a rag in her hand, she said, "Well, you were in my way."

"You're rude."

She gave me no response. She was obviously one of those girls — all talk and no action.

After watch, I went to berthing to go to sleep. Smith followed me.

"Taylor," she said. "Chief told me that they're both being written up and taken to captain's mast. Will you support me and tell the board what's been happening in CIC while on watch? Will you tell them about the name-calling?"

"Of course I will," I answered her. "If this happened to me, I would expect you to speak up for me."

That seemed to soothe her and we both fell asleep.

The next day, I woke up a few hours early and went outside for some fresh air. I leaned over the side, looking down at the waves crashing against the ship. Williams came and stood right next to me.

He looked at me and said, "How are you doing?"

"Fine," I answered looking back. "I miss my daughter a lot and I miss my family. Sometimes I don't know why I joined. There's also a lot of fighting going on in my watch section."

"I know what you mean about missing your daughter. I have a son that's three years old. I miss him a lot, too."

Just then, he reached into his pocket and pulled out his wallet. Opening it up, he pulled out a picture of his son. His son looked just like him — blond hair, big, blue eyes, and a big smile to match.

"He's cute," I said. "He looks like you. I'll have to show you a picture of my daughter. I don't have one on me."

As the setting sun cast rainbows in the sky, we talked about family and children and the long days out at sea. It was nice to have someone friendly to talk to and we both had a lot in common. I told Williams I'd see him later and then I headed down to watch.

As I entered CIC, Green was getting off of watch and told me to meet her and Chief in tactical logistics (TACLOG) for an evaluation. TACLOG is a place on the ship used for combat meetings. Since I was new, I hadn't had an evaluation done yet. I still didn't know what TACLOG was, so I thought I'd better follow Green. As we entered a room with a cipher lock on it, I saw Chief sitting in a chair. Green sat in the chair next to him. I assumed I was supposed to sit in the single chair in front of them. They both discussed what was expected of me as an OS, training material I had to complete on deployment, as well as my goals for being in the navy. I told them that I wanted to be an officer. I would be working on my package to send out while I was on deployment. I told them that I'd appreciate it if they could look over my package and give me any ideas on how to improve it. They both agreed that becoming an officer was a good goal and told me they'd take a look once I had everything together.

For years, my goal had been to become an officer. Initially, before I joined the navy, I'd trained for a year to go into the Marine Corps Officers Program. I'd never worked so mentally and physically hard in my life. Since I was an older candidate, I'd even gone back to high school to retake my SATs since the scores had changed since I graduated. I also worked out with the marines three times a week either running or lifting weights. Sadly, my package was denied because they felt that I was too old to go and that I might suffer from stress fractures. I felt devastated. I'd put in all of that hard work for nothing. Being the strong-willed person that I am, I decided to take the Officer Aptitude Rating (OAR) exam with the navy. After passing with a good score, I put my package together to apply for Officer Candidate School (OCS). Of course, I was denied again. This was my third attempt. I'd always heard that the third time's a charm, so maybe this would be my chance.

Before going back on watch, Chief told me that the next morning when I got off watch at 0700 I was to report to the chiefs' mess hall for captain's mast. I knew what it was about; the blood on the pillow incident. I told him I would be there. The chiefs' mess hall was where all of the chiefs on the ship ate their meals. Just as the officers on ship had their own mess hall in which to eat, so did the lower ranks.

Watch stayed very quiet that evening. No one said a word unless it was work-related. Flannery and Nicolette remained quiet. They didn't even talk to each other. They both knew what was in store the next morning. While sitting on the radar inside CIC, trying to stay awake, I heard a masculine voice.

"Hey, would you like some trail mix?"

To my right stood a man with dark, blond hair and a nice tan. He appeared to be around his thirties. He smiled as held out a huge bag of trail mix.

"Sure," I said smiling. After all, maybe eating would help me to stay awake. "I've seen you in here before talking to Smith. What do you do?"

"FC1 Matthews," he said. "I'm a fire controlman. I operate weapons systems onboard surface combatant ships."

"Oh," I answered, not really understanding what he'd just said.

"How do you like it so far?" he asked.

"Well, I miss my family and I'm still getting used to the job," I responded.

Matthews offered me more trail mix.

"If you need anything, let me know. Also, don't tell anyone," Matthews said, lowering his voice. "If you ever need any coffee, I make my own in my office. You're welcome to have some. Smith is the only other person allowed to have any."

"Thanks! That would be great." I was ecstatic to hear that.

Twenty minutes later, I looked up from the radar to see Matthews standing next to me holding out a cup of coffee. He brought cream and sugar in case I used any. I gave him a smile and he smiled back. As he got back to work in CIC, I noticed that he sat in the back of the room in the position of gunnery liaison officer (GLO). *What a nice man,* I thought to myself. *I guess there are still some nice people in this world.*

Having been relieved from watch, I headed down to the chiefs' mess and saw Smith, Vale, Nicolette, and Flannery standing in the p-way outside. I found it interesting that Vale was standing there since she was in the other watch section. I didn't think she knew anything about what was going on. Chief came walking down the p-way headed toward us. He told us that no one should be talking. Then he opened the door to the mess and told Flannery and Nicolette to follow him inside. Vale whispered, "I saw them smear the blood on her pillow."

"I'm down here because I heard the mean things they were saying to Smith," I whispered.

No sooner had I finished telling Vale why I was there than I heard voices yelling inside the room. I was scared to go in and I hadn't even done anything.

The door opened and Chief sent Flannery and Nicolette to wait down the p-way. Chief told Smith to come inside. No one spoke. After waiting about ten minutes, the door opened and Chief sent out Smith. It was Vale's turn. I knew that speaking up was the right thing to do, even if Flannery and Nicolette hated me. Opening the door again, Vale was told that she was free to go. It was time for me to go inside. A long table stood at the front of the room. At the table sat CDR Vermont, LCDR Dennis, and CMC Weiss. CDR Vermont looked very intimidating. He was a very tall, white man with light-brown hair. He was stocky in build and had a stern look on his face.

He asked in an assertive voice, "What did you witness while on watch in CIC?"

I told him that I'd heard them talking badly about Smith, saying that she stank and didn't shower. I said that I was with Smith when she found the blood on her pillow. I said that I didn't know who did it, but I did know that the three of them were having problems. I didn't know, however, why they didn't like each other.

LCDR Dennis looked at me and smiled, and then he told me I was free to go. He had a friendlier face when he smiled. Looks can be deceiving. Just because someone appears nice doesn't mean that they actually are nice. Dennis had a slight build. His hair was blond and the tips were a little curly. Though I wasn't sure how old he was, he appeared younger than the others. I was proud of myself for speaking up for Smith. I left the room knowing I had done the right thing.

Since I didn't feel very tired, I decided to take the opportunity to go the gym before going to sleep for the night. The gym was very relaxing. I was the only one there. I enjoyed being alone and listening to the music on my MP3 player. After working out for forty-five minutes, I went to take a shower and get ready for bed. Before going into my berthing, I went into BFFT to see if I could get on a computer to check my e-mail. No one was in BFFT so I was able to get on a computer. I had one message from John.

Hey, haven't heard from you. I don't know if I can handle this. I feel neglected. I can't eat or sleep. I don't know what you're doing. Please let me know if we're still OK.

I replied.

How are you doing? What do you mean you don't think you can handle this? I handled things when you were gone with the marines. I've only been gone three weeks. You still have a long way to go. I'm very busy on the ship learning my job. I'll try to write and call when I can. Everything is fine. Try not to worry.

After waking up with an hour before going on watch, I got dressed, got a quick bite to eat, and headed outside for fresh air. Heading up past the smoke deck, I found a rail away from other people. Just as I began to think of my family and my home, Chief came up to ask how I was doing.

"I'm doing OK," I said. "I'm just thinking about Aria."

I told Chief that she was a dancer and that I also liked to dance and knew many different styles. I told him I'd done tap, jazz, ballet, Irish, and belly dancing.

"Really," he said, sounding very interested. "I'd like to see you belly dance sometime. I bet you'd look really good in a belly-dancer's outfit." He leaned in close to me and his shoulder leaned lightly against mine. "You know, you're a very attractive woman."

Had I heard him correctly? It sounded like the chief was coming on to me. He continued to lean into me, staring down at my chest before making eye contact. I didn't know what to say.

"Oh, well, thank you," I blurted out. "I better get ready to go on watch."

I pushed myself away from the railing and turned to head down the stairs.

"I'll see you in there," he responded.

Walking to go on watch, I felt very uncomfortable but wondered if I might be overreacting. After all, he was my boss. He had a family of his own. So I convinced myself that it was nothing. He was just being nice—wasn't he?

CHAPTER FIVE

Wog Day

Time passed slowly. It was only the end of November. I'd been hearing talk on the ship about Wog Day, which was coming up. We'd be crossing the equator on our way to the Mariana Islands, which includes Guam and Saipan. Sailors who had never crossed the equator before were called wogs (short for pollywog). Those who had crossed the equator before would have different events in which they would torture the wogs for a few hours out on the flight deck. I, unlike the others, wasn't looking forward to it. Lately, I'd been feeling really tired and had no energy. The last thing I wanted to do was run around the ship being tortured. I'd been suffering from a sore throat and a runny nose. Every time I went to blow my nose, it hurt every part of my face. I also noticed thick, green mucous. I knew I had a sinus infection. I felt worse and worse as the days went by. Though I hated to go down to medical, I thought that I'd better go and see if they could give me something. I saw Hospital Corpsman (HM) 1 Reece. He told me to sit down so that he could take my temperature.

"You have a fever of one hundred and one," he said looking at the thermometer. "It looks like you have a sinus infection. Give me a moment while I go talk to Senior Chief Knight."

I'd never spoken to Senior Chief Knight before, but I knew that he was in charge of medical. He was a roly-poly guy with a Hitler-like mustache. When Reece returned, he said that they couldn't give me any antibiotics, but he would give me some Tylenol. Since I've suffered from sinus infections my whole life, I knew that Tylenol wouldn't help.

"I need antibiotics," I told him, "or it will just get worse."

He just stared at me, so I grabbed my medication and started to leave.

"Hold on," he said.

He walked away and when he returned I noticed he had a small bag in his hands with little, white pills.

"Here," he said acting secretive. "Take these antibiotics. Keep them in your rack and don't tell anyone that I gave them to you."

In a hurry, I took the bag, said thank you, and ran up to berthing to take my first dose. Since I had a fever, medical had given me a chit to stay in berthing for a couple of days. Before returning to work, I had to get checked out first. Giving Chief the medical note, he appeared annoyed, but had to let me go to berthing. He told me I'd be missing Wog Day. I told him that I understood but felt horrible.

That night was awful. I could not sleep. My pillow was so flat and every time I tried to sleep, the mucous would drain down my throat. I got up in the middle of the night to use the bathroom. I figured that no one would be out in the p-way and walked around that way to get to the head. As soon as I opened the door to berthing, I ran into a young electronics technician (ET).

"Oh, sorry," I said.

"That's OK," he responded. "You scared me. I haven't seen you on the ship. Are you new?"

"Yes," I answered. "Sorry. I've been sick in bed all day. It's been hard for me to sleep. I wish I had a better pillow."

"I have a nice, feather pillow that my parents sent me if you'd like to borrow it. It might make you sleep better," he said sympathetically. "Wait here. I'll be right back."

When he returned, he had a big, down pillow in his hands. He introduced himself as ET2 Erikson. He was very young and good-looking. He had sky-blue eyes. I could tell that he had a lazy eye that wandered. I couldn't believe he was going to let me borrow his pillow. I'd be getting my germs all over it. I told him that it was a very nice gesture and that I would give him his pillow back once I got better. He told me it was no rush, he was happy to meet me, and that he would see me around the ship.

Wog Day arrived. As I lay in bed, I watched the women in my berthing getting ready. They'd taken white shirts and cut them up. Then they wrote "Wog" on the front and back. Those who would be doing the torturing dressed as pirates. Soon after, everyone left and I was the only person who remained. Hours passed. Just as I finally started to doze off, the door to berthing flung open and I was woken by a bunch of loud, soaked females. Smith was one of the first to enter.

"How are you feeling?" she asked.

"Better, but still stuffed up," I told her. "How was it?"

"I wish you'd done it. It was so much fun. They made us pretend we were in rowboats and as we were rowing, they had the hose turned on spraying us with water. Everyone's soaked."

Wishing I'd received a certificate for passing Wog Day, I felt disappointed. I knew that if I'd participated, though, I would've just gotten worse.

Tired of lying in bed, the next morning I went down to medical to be checked out. They told me I was good to go back on watch. Walking out of medical, I ran into Chief and told him I would be back on watch that night. Since I'd missed Wog Day for legitimately being sick, he handed me a certificate that said I'd passed. Then he told me he'd see me on watch. I thought about what he'd said about belly dancing and finding me attractive. I knew that I'd overreacted. It was nice of him to give me a certificate even though I hadn't participated.

A few days later, the Russiantown docked in Guam. It was a beautiful, lush, and green island. It reminded me of a TV show that was on in the seventies called *Fantasy Island*. I wasn't sure who I'd be joining on liberty. Since we would only be there a short while, the command instructed us to stay on base, but we could attend a club on base that had dancing and music. I dressed in civilian clothes and then headed out into the p-way where I ran into Montgomery. He told me that he, Schuemaker, Richards, and Davis were going to grab beers and hang out at a park on base. He invited me to come along. Since I didn't have any plans, I accepted the invitation.

Walking off the ship, we ran into some other guys and signed out on liberty together. Even though I was the only girl, I felt comfortable. Montgomery, who was a heavy drinker, wanted to stop at the store right away to get beer. Once we reached the park, we gave each other a toast. Montgomery toasted to being at our first port and being off the ship. The night was exactly what I needed. We laughed and made jokes. It felt like someone had put laughing gas in our drinks. From a distance we could hear the music and see the lights from the club. Out of curiosity, we decided to head over to check it out. The place was packed. People danced and a lot of the sailors were already drunk.

"Taylor! Over here!" I could see a young girl waving. It was Smith. She was with her boyfriend, a BM3 on the ship.

"Hey," I said.

"Who are you here with?" she asked.

I pointed to the guys. "Montgomery, Schuemaker, Richards, and Davis."

Looking over at Schuemaker, I could tell he'd already had too much to drink. He could barely stand and looked like he was going to puke.

"I'll see you on ship," I told Smith. "Schuemaker isn't looking so good. I think I'll get him back. I don't want him to get into trouble."

Walking over to Schuemaker, I told the others I'd take him back since they weren't yet ready to leave. Walking out of the club, I let Schuemaker put most of his weight on me. Since he was so thin, he didn't feel that heavy. The hard part was his height. Just before we reached the bus stop, he got sick and threw up in the bushes. It was disgusting. At least it helped him to feel better. Plus, it was better to throw up on base rather than on the ship.

Once we got to the ship, I managed to get us both signed in and walked him up the stairs to his berthing area. Since I couldn't go in male berthing, I opened the door to let him in, hoping he would make it to the right bed. Walking to my berthing, I felt glad to be back and ready to get a good night's sleep. Tomorrow would be a long day with two sea and anchor stations. First, we would leave Guam by 0800. Then we would travel to Saipan to dock in the evening, which meant getting off the ship again. This time, we'd be there for three days. That meant we'd get two days of liberty and one day of twenty-four-hour watch on the ship.

At 0800, sea and anchor was set. I was told I'd be on the bridge. I headed up to the bridge where I'd be working with the navigation officer and the QMs. Erikson was also on the bridge. He was waiting to talk to me.

"Taylor, do you have a liberty buddy to go with in Saipan?" he asked.

"No," I said, surprised by his question. "Not yet. Why?"

"Well, I don't have anyone to go with. I didn't get off the ship in Guam and I really want to look around Saipan. Will you go with me for the day?"

Though I didn't know him that well, he had let me borrow his pillow. He seemed liked a nice person. I was ready to get off the ship.

"Sure," I said. "I'll go with you tomorrow."

With a smile on his face, he told me he'd meet me at my berthing at 0830.

Once we docked in Saipan, a muster was held with all OSs to talk to everyone about behaving themselves while on liberty. Afterward, I put on my sweats and went outside for some fresh air before going to sleep. This time I went up to the 07 level. I sat on a small box that overlooked the whole front end of the ship. I folded my arms and rested my chin on my hands. It felt good to have some peace and quiet. Around thirty minutes passed and as I was getting ready to go back inside berthing to go to sleep, a man's voice startled me.

"Hi. Haven't seen you in a while."

Turning around, I saw that it was Williams.

"Hi," I answered. "I haven't seen you either. How was Guam?"

"It was OK. Just a bunch of the guys getting drunk." He spoke to me as if I was one of the guys and knew just what that felt like. "Are you going out in Saipan?"

"Yes," I answered.

"Do you maybe want to go out on liberty together one day?" he asked.

"I guess so. I'm already going out with someone the first day, though. Maybe the second day," I said, thinking his request was strange. He seemed nice, but I hoped he didn't have an ulterior motive.

"Sounds good," he said. He told me that he'd meet me the second day in front of my berthing around 0800. Watching him walk away, I felt excited that I could finally get off the ship to do some shopping.

The next morning, Erikson was waiting right outside berthing at 0830. After walking off the ship, we talked about what we felt like doing. He wanted to go to the beach. I wanted to see the beach as well, but I was hoping he wouldn't want to go out in the water. During muster the night before, the division was told to watch out for barracudas in the water. That's all I needed; to run into the water and have my foot bitten off.

On the way to the beach, I decided to stop at a bathing suit store to buy a cover-up. Looking through each and every dress, I could tell that Erikson was getting antsy to get to the beach. I decided on a pink, flowery dress.

We must have walked at least three or four miles before getting to the beach. Once we got there, I had to admit that it was gorgeous. The sand was as white as could be. The water looked so blue and clear. I could see all of the sea life under the water. Already stripped down to his swim trunks, Erikson took off running toward the water. I wasn't as willing to run and frolic. I kept thinking of barracudas, sharks, and fish in the water touching me. I am not an outdoorsy kind of girl.

"Come on," Erikson yelled at me.

The water felt warm and the sand felt soft. Walking out into the water, I could feel something spongy on my feet. I looked down into the water and saw something jet black and as big as a potato.

"I keep walking on something spongy," I yelled to Erikson.

"They're just sea slugs," he yelled back. "They won't hurt you."

I stood frozen in the water. Erikson came over and told me to grab his shoulders and get on his back so that he could take me out into the water. I told him that I was scared because I couldn't swim that well, but he told me to trust him.

"See," he said, walking away from the shore. "It's not even deep."

As soon as the words escaped his mouth, we both sank under the water. In a panic, I let go and left him in the deep water. I tried to dog-paddle back to shore. In my harried state, I accidently kicked him in the head while trying to swim. Within a few seconds, I felt hands grab me on my waist. He told me to grab on to his shoulders. I wrapped my arms around his neck and my legs around his torso. Poor guy. I could only imagine the extra weight he carried while trying to walk to shore. As we reached the shore, I realized that I was no longer on his back; I was looking at him eye-to-eye. I'd been hanging on to the front of him like a monkey. After unlatching myself, I apologized. Luckily, he saw the humor and started laughing. He confirmed that I had kicked him in the head. I played it off like I didn't know, laughing and acting shocked. That was enough swimming for us for the day.

For the next hour, Erikson and I looked for shells on the beach and walked around the shops. Once night fell, we got a nice dinner at Tony Roma's and then walked back to the ship. Of course, since we'd gone out on liberty together, people had started to talk. They thought that maybe we were dating. People can be so immature. As soon as a man is spotted with a woman having fun, it's automatically assumed that they're dating. For us, it was merely a nice time spent with a new friend. We were both so tired from the long day that we got back to the ship before 2200. Stepping outside, I called home.

"Hello?" My mom answered the phone.

"Hey, Mom. Is John there?"

"No, he's not here right now," she said.

"Where is he?" I asked.

"He's at work right now. I'll let him know that you called. You know, it's weird but I've been noticing things missing from the bedroom. Remember that wooden chest that John had?"

"Yes," I said.

"Well, that's gone along with some of his clothes and his metal filing box."

"Really?" I agreed with my mom that it was strange that things were missing. I told her that John had sent me a weird e-mail about not being able to eat or sleep and about not being able to handle the deployment. I told her that I would forward the e-mail to her and that if he sent anymore, I would send them to her to keep. I felt like something was wrong. I wanted to keep the e-mails in case anything happened and I needed them later. I didn't know what the future would hold.

After a good night's sleep on the ship, I woke and was ready by 0830 to go on liberty with Williams. He was waiting for me outside my berthing. Leaving the ship for another day on Saipan, I asked Williams what he wanted to do. I should have known when he said he wanted to go to the beach. While walking there, we noticed an outside food market. The smell of food in the air was amazing. There were so many different aromas of spices that made my mouth water. Since we were both hungry, we decided to get some lunch. One of the stands I saw was selling chow mein and chicken that looked delicious. Everything was so fresh. Williams chose to order the same. Since there were no tables or chairs, we popped a squat right on the curb and watched the locals eating the variety of food from the stands. Enjoying our meal, we laughed and talked about the different people on the ship. I felt very comfortable, perhaps too comfortable. I started to mention what my Chief had said about wanting to see me belly dance and finding me attractive.

"He said that to you?" Williams responded looking concerned. "That's really inappropriate."

"Well, he hasn't said anything since then," I said.

"As long as he doesn't say anything else."

"Well, I hope he doesn't. I just got to this command and I don't want to start any problems. I'm going for my officer package for the third time and really want it. I don't want anything to stand in my way."

"How much more until you are ready to send in your package?" he asked.

"I have all my recommendations. What I really need to do is my CO essay. I plan to have everything done in a couple months. I need to make sure I have it in to make this next selection board." I answered.

Looking at eachother, we noticed that we were both finished with our food.

We threw our plates in the trash and headed for the beach.

Of course, Williams wanted to go in the water, but I remembered how things had gone the day before with Erikson. Since I felt scared of the water, I let Williams walk out and swim. When he returned, we walked the beach looking for shells.

"Wow! Look at that shell over there!" Williams exclaimed.

I ran over to see the shell he found. It was a gigantic, abalone shell that was in perfect condition. The only problem was that it smelled of fish. Even though it smelled foul, Williams wanted to keep it as a souvenir.

As the day went on, Williams and I had a lot of fun together. We went shopping and hung out at the Marriott in Saipan. We didn't know what else to do with ourselves and we didn't want to go back to the ship yet. After having a drink at the bar, we noticed a Ping-Pong table in the courtyard of the hotel. We must have spent an hour playing. It was still somewhat light out when we started. By the time we finished, it was dark outside.

"What do you want to do next?" Williams asked.

"How about we go walk around outside and maybe go to a club for a little bit."

"Sounds good."

Walking around Saipan at night was like being in another universe. What happened to the Saipan I'd seen during the day? All of the food places and the stores changed into brothels and special massage places. By special massage places I mean places where women took care of the men's needs. Prostitutes walked the streets everywhere. They wore super short and tight dresses with heels that had to be at least five to six inches. I love heels myself, but I couldn't imagine walking the streets all night in those things. While Williams and I were walking across a crosswalk, a prostitute ran out of nowhere and pinched Williams on the butt. Looking surprised, he turned around just in time to pull her arms off of him. She was just like a leach. She didn't want to let go and kept telling him to come with her so she could show him a good time. She was very thin with long, black hair. She wore more makeup than a clown at the circus, and her eyelashes were so gobbed with mascara that it looked like a spider had died on her face. She looked sick. Williams finally got her to let go.

We proceeded down a street with a lot of clubs and bars. We went into one of the dance clubs and everyone from the ship was there. Of course, a lot of people were already drunk. I saw Montgomery, Schuemaker, Richards, and Davis. Since Williams didn't want to dance, Montgomery and I went out on the dance floor to break it down. Montgomery tried so hard to dance, bless his soul, but he was pretty intoxicated. Cutting our dancing short, I took him back to his seat. Williams asked me if I would like anything to drink.

"Sure," I said. "You buy this time and I'll buy next time."

While Williams went and got us something to drink, some of his marine friends came over and joined us. They all seemed really nice. Feeling that someone was staring at me, I saw Chief Weinerbangher hanging out with the other chiefs from the ship. I decided to get up and go talk to him.

"Hi, Chief. Are you enjoying yourself?" I asked.

"I went and had a special massage. It was nice. You look nice," he said with a drink in his hand. Then he leaned in to me and said, "Hey, why don't you ditch that person you're with and come with me for the night?"

"I can't do that," I said, sounding shocked. "He's my liberty buddy and I need to stay with him. I'll see you back on the ship. Have a fun night." Clearly, he was drunk.

As I walked back, Williams could tell that something had happened. I guess the look on my face had given it away.

"What did he tell you?" I could hear the seriousness in his voice.

"He told me to ditch you and to come with him for the night," I told him.

"What a bastard!" Williams said angrily. "Do you want me to go say something to him?"

"No!" I shouted. "Leave it alone. He's probably had a lot to drink."

Williams asked if I was ready to leave to go back to the ship. I told him I was ready. Walking the dark streets, we both heard a man's voice behind us. Turning around, we saw that it was Gunnery Sergeant Rodrigo. I first met Rodrigo through my husband. He is one ugly guy. No kidding. He is also weird. Mid-conversation with Rodrigo, all of a sudden, he'd stop talking, put his head down, and make the sign of the cross. One day, I asked him why. He told me he'd felt a bad presence surrounding him and did it to ward off the evil spirit. But for someone so religious, he sure liked women. I could just tell by the way he eyeballed them. It was quiet apparent that he'd forgotten what he learned in sexual harassment training.

Slurring his words, Rodrigo grabbed my arm. "Yeah, you. Do you want to get it on with me? We could all have a threesome."

Taking his hand off of me, I responded, "You're drunk. I don't think so."

As we picked up our pace to lose him, Rodrigo just kept following behind while yelling.

"Hey! I said I want to have sex with you. I know you want to."

"Go away!" I yelled back.

Williams suggested that we run ahead and then go down a different street. As we ran, we could still hear him yelling. I know they say never leave a shipmate behind, but Rodrigo was a pig. He was not a shipmate.

Finally, we made it back to the ship and signed in. Williams walked me to my berthing and told me he'd had a good time. I told him that I'd had fun as well. Climbing into my rack, I thought to myself, *How much more can I take? I still have a long time out to sea.* I closed my eyes thinking of home and eventually I fell asleep.

CHAPTER SIX

Straits of Hormuz

S ea and anchor detail took place first thing in the morning so that we could leave Saipan to head to the Middle East. Once we got there, we'd be out to sea most of the time. The deployment was intended to protect the oil rigs and to train with navy members living on the rigs. Days and nights passed per usual. It felt like the movie Groundhog Day; every day seemed the same. On certain days, I would run on the flight deck before watch. I figured that would change things up some since I typically went to the gym. Running on the flight deck was challenging because the ship rocked. It was kind of fun. Every time the ship rocked to the left, I would fall over to the left of the ship; when it rocked right, I would fall over to the right. Thank goodness there were nets around the ship so that if I fell off, I wouldn't land in the ocean.

Since we hadn't been into port for more than sixty days, the CO issued a beer day on the flight deck. Each sailor was issued two bottles of beer. Once they finished, they could either go back to work or go back to what they'd been doing elsewhere. McGraw, who loved to drink beer, felt upset that she wouldn't get to go. She was on watch. Because I didn't care whether I went or not, I offered to relieve her early if she would relieve me early the next morning. McGraw was so excited, especially to get out of CIC. As I assumed my place on watch, I felt happy for her to get to drink beer and enjoy herself. I also felt happy to get off before the others.

Christmas drew near. It was already the beginning of December. Personally, I didn't want to be reminded that it was Christmas time. I think the others felt the same. For one thing, every morning the CO played Christmas music, which I found to be really annoying. Within CIC, there were a few people that felt the spirit of the holidays. They decorated CIC with Christmas lights and a small, sad, Charlie Brown tree in the corner of the room. The only things I looked forward to were packages sent by my family. Everything else seemed meaningless. Why celebrate Christmas when it would be a regular work day just like any other day out to sea?

One night while standing watch, I noticed Chief Weinerbangher staring at me while I was working at the radar. He got up from his chair and walked over. The more I looked at him, the more he reminded me of Shrek. He looked like a big ogre. Hopping up on the chart table next to me, he made sure to sit extra close and leaned over.

"How are you doing? How is your officer package coming along?"

"It's coming along. It's a lot of work. I'm just working on the CO's essay," I said.

"I would like to talk to you in private," he said.

Assuming it was about my officer package, I agreed, but found it strange that we had to talk in private.

"It would look too conspicuous for both of us to leave now," Chief said quietly in my ear. "I'll leave first and then I'll call for you."

He jumped off of the chart table and walked out of the room. Behind me, Smith and Campbell were watching. Neither one of them said anything. They just stared.

About twenty minutes later, Chief telephoned Campbell and requested that I go up to TACLOG. Campbell told me to go and then told Smith to take the radar while he worked the DDRT.

Entering TACLOG, I saw the Chief sitting in a chair. He'd pulled up another chair right in front of him. I asked if he wanted me to go get my officer package, but he said it wasn't necessary. I walked over to the chair next to him and sat down.

I could tell he wanted to say something. His lips parted, but they never formed a word. It seemed as though he was hesitating to tell me something. I felt nervous because I thought I might be in trouble.

"You are a very attractive woman," Chief whispered. "I find myself very attracted to you." He grabbed my right hand and held it in his.

I didn't say a thing. I didn't know what to say. I felt the soft strokes of his hand on top of mine.

He proceeded. "You know, my wife and I have been having problems and things have been hard for me. We don't talk anymore and haven't been close for a long time. I find myself having feelings for you and I can't hide them. What are we going to do about these feelings? I know you have them also. I can see it in your eyes. I don't know what to do about my marriage. The only thing that's keeping me from leaving my wife is our son."

"I...well....everyone has some problems in marriage," I stuttered. I didn't know what to say.

Just then, he grabbed onto my arms and firmly held me close while he leaned in to force a kiss on me. His lips were cold and slimy. I push back again his chest with my hands to get him to move away from me. It didn't seem to phase him. He didn't notice that I wasn't excepting his actions.

"Now we need to keep this a secret just between you and me," Chief continued. "I would get into a lot of trouble if they found out about us. You would get into trouble as well. I know you're trying to get into the officer program and if anyone found out, it might hurt your chances."

Was this guy delusional? In his mind, he had a relationship with me. As he held my right hand, he asked how my package was going. I told him that I was still working on it and should have it done soon. I told him how important it was for me to become an officer and that it was a goal of mine.

"If you need anything," Chief said, "remember I am here for you. You better get back on watch. People will get suspicious. I don't want them to think anything because I called you out of watch."

Walking out of the room, I felt sick to my stomach. He was my boss. I was the low person on the totem pole. If I brought this to anyone's attention, it would cause waves. Chief also had a lot of other chiefs as friends on the ship; they would all back him up. I had my officer package at stake. That was my reason for joining the navy. Besides, Chief would be leaving soon. In a few months, he would be leaving to go to another command and we would get a new OSC.

When I entered CIC, Smith and Campbell stared at me. I took my place back on the radar. After getting off watch, Smith asked why Chief had called me out and why I'd been gone so long. I told her to go to BFFT and I would tell her. When I did tell her, she looked shocked, but not surprised. She told me that he was known for liking women and this type of thing had happened to two other OSs on the ship before I came on board.

Smith leaned forward to me and whispered, "There was a girl here right before you came named OS2 Dupree. Chief was always around her and she got special treatment. She could never do anything wrong. I can't tell you for sure what happened between them. And she wasn't the only girl he had feelings for on the ship. He's bothered others and it always gets swept under the rug. You should just be careful."

I was surprised that such behavior had been going on and that no one had ever done anything about it. I made Smith promise that she wouldn't say a word to anyone. I told her I didn't want to cause any waves. She agreed, but told me that if it got worse or happened again, I had better say something.

The next morning, I went for another run on the flight deck and did crunches at the gym. As I lay on the gym floor with my arms behind my head, Williams came up to me.

"Hey, stranger. I haven't seen you on the 06 level lately. Movie night's tonight out on the flight deck for Christmas Eve. It starts before you go on watch. They're supposed to have popcorn. Meet me down there."

"Sounds good," I responded. "I will meet you down there. I won't be able to stay too long, though, because I have to be on watch at seven."

Smiling, I told Williams I was going to get some sleep. He told me he was going to lift weights. Heading up to the berthing, I still felt bothered by what had happened with the chief. I wished I could call my parents, but every time the phones were up and working, I had duty. I knew that e-mailing wouldn't be a good idea; that would involve putting information out for the whole world to see. Besides, e-mail was down.

That evening before watch, I went down to meet Williams. He was there with some of his marine friends. I didn't mind his friends because they were all very nice and respectful. The feature film for the night was *Cars*. Williams had gotten me some popcorn. The stars were so bright and vivid that night. It felt like I could reach up into the sky and touch them with my hand. Looking over to Williams who was busy watching the movie, I felt as though I could confide in him. I could trust him. We'd spent evenings talking and confiding in each other about our problems and our insecurities. He'd become one of my closest friends.

"It happened again," I told him.

"What happened?"

"Chief said something to me again. This time he pulled me out of watch and took me to a room where he forced me to kiss him. He told me that he had feelings for me and that he could tell I was feeling the same way toward him. He spoke about leaving his wife but that he was worried because of his son." Hesitating, I continued. "He told me not to tell anyone. He also started to talk to me about my officer package. He said that if anyone found out, we'd both be in trouble and it would jeopardize my officer package. I don't know what to do."

"What?" Williams said, outraged. "You have to say something to someone. You can't let him get away with this. This is sexual harassment. He could get into a lot of trouble for this. You won't get into trouble."

"I'm afraid to say anything because I don't want to mess up my chances of going to OCS," I told him.

"He's wrong. I'm telling you that this is a dangerous situation," Williams exclaimed.

"I know," I told him. "I know."

Looking at my wristwatch, I saw that I only had a couple of minutes to get to watch. I told Williams I'd see him later. I knew that our discussion was far from over. Williams always knew what to say to make me feel better. He gave me good advice. Williams asked if I'd be down at mid-rats later that night. He said he'd wait up to talk to me on the mess decks. Nodding in agreement, I headed off to CIC.

That night, watch went by pretty quickly. Chief was in CIC for a little while, but then he left to go to the operations office. Supposedly, he'd been taking some classes online. Around 0200, Campbell told me he needed to have some secret documents shredded and asked me to go to the operations office to do so. Of all places, that was one I did not want to visit. I knew that Chief was in there. I grabbed the bag of paper from Campbell and took off down the p-way.

When I entered the office, I saw Chief talking to FCC Lard. She was the chief in charge of the weapons division and the fattest chief I had ever seen other than mine. I wondered to myself, *How in the world did they pass their PRTs?* The test consisted of running a mile and a half, then doing push-ups and sit-ups. Someone on the ship must have fixed their scores. I couldn't even imagine them getting off the ground. FCC Lard was short with dark-brown hair that she always wore slicked back. She wore her hair so tight that you could see the fat rolls in the back of her head beneath her bun. She had a look on her face like she always smelled poo. Her uniform was way too small. I've seen camel toe in my life, but nothing like this. Camel toe is slang for wearing tight clothing on a womans labia majora. Gotta love those scientific words. In lame man terms, it is a woman's front private part. When split in two, it is said to resemble a camels forefoot. Lard's camels toe superseded the forefoot of a camel and resembled a taco that had been overstuffed. It had to hurt. That must be what made her such an unpleasant woman. She must have been in constant pain. As much as I tried not to look in that direction, my eyes were drawn there.

"What do you want?" she asked me with a nasty tone in her voice.

"OS2 Campbell sent me to shred," I said, looking at both her and Chief.

"Fine," she said. "Make sure you clean the machine when you're done."

I sat at the shredder where Lard looked me up and down. It was the type of moment where I wanted to let out a loud fart to break the silence, especially since she was such a mean and nasty individual. I imagined doing so and started to laugh a little, but quickly stopped myself and put on a serious face. Leaving the room, Lard told Chief good night and left to go get some sleep. For a while, Chief sat and did his schoolwork while I shredded. Just before I'd finished up the shredding, he carried his chair over and sat right next to me.

"We're going to be in Bahrain in a couple of days. I want us to get a hotel room together. I've been thinking of having sex with you for days now. Every night when I go to sleep, I dream about you. Remember, we need to be discreet if we get a room. No one can see us."

Slowly, he removed his hands from his lap and started massaging my neck.

"I can't wait to see you out of your coveralls," he said, moving his hands from my neck to my shoulders. A chill ran down my spine instantly.

Looking right at him, I said, "I don't think that's a good idea."

I moved away and told him that I had to finish shredding. He said he understood and we'd talk about making plans and getting a hotel room later. As I watched him get up to go, I wondered if he had mental problem. He just didn't understand that I was not interested.

At this point, I was really shaken up. I just wanted to go home. Was this what the navy was all about? I realized that it wasn't the navy's fault, but I couldn't believe that a man with years of service would be acting this way.

That night at mid-rats, I went down to eat with Smith. Williams sat at one of the tables. I introduced him to Smith. As they started a conversation about being on the ship and work, Richards came up with a friend of his, Hull Technician (HT) Farland.

Richards asked me, "Do you have a liberty buddy when we get to Bahrain?"

I smiled and said, "No, do you want to go together?"

"Well, is it OK if Farland comes, too?"

"Sure," I agreed.

I didn't know Farland that well, but he seemed nice. They both got up from the table and headed back to work. Looking over, I saw that Williams was smiling.

"Aren't we popular."

I knew he was kidding. I could tell by the grin on his face. He was teasing me and giving me a hard time about the fact that Williams and I had become such good friends. Smith just started laughing. I asked Williams who he was going into town with. He told me he'd go with some of the guys. Smith told me she'd be going with her boyfriend and FC1 Matthews. Realizing that Smith and I only had five minutes to get back on watch, I told Williams I'd see him later.

That night on watch, Matthews came up to Smith and I and asked if we'd like some coffee. I told him I could definitely use some. I turned to Campbell and asked him if I could go for coffee. He told me it was fine, but to hurry back.

Following Matthews, I entered his office in a rush. Sure enough, he had a coffee pot set up and his laptop was set on a ledge near a black case filled with movies.

"Wow, you have a lot of movies," I told him. "There are some good ones in here, too."

Laughing a little, he replied, "You're welcome in here any-time you want to watch a movie. I also keep a stash of snacks."

"I'll take you up on that offer."

I thought to myself, *How cool is this?* Matthews offered a place to get away and watch a movie. Besides, Matthews and I had become close friends. We had a lot in common. We were the same age, listened to a lot of the same music, and could carry on a nice, long conversation. I could tell that he was also a person I could trust.

Picking up the coffee, Matthews turned to me and said, "Smith told me that Chief Weinerbangher was bothering you and making sexual advances."

I was stunned. I looked at him like a deer in headlights.

"Please don't say anything. He'll be leaving anyway. I don't want to create waves," I answered while walking out of the office. I think he could tell that I didn't want to talk about it anymore.

Once I got back into CIC, I handed Smith her coffee. I wanted to confront her to ask why she told Matthews, but Campbell said it was time to rotate and I needed to go up to the bridge. Entering the bridge, it took a few moments for my eyes to adjust to the darkness. I made it to the radar and then took the phones from Nicolette. A few minutes after I took over watch, the bridge door opened on the starboard side by my radar. Starboard on a ship is the right side. The left side is called port.

"Hi," said someone in a deep voice. "I came up to see you before I go on watch."

I squinted my eyes to try to see who it was.

"Who is this?" I asked.

"It's Erikson."

"How are you?" I asked. "I haven't seen you in a while."

"I've been working a lot. Well, I just came up to say hi. I better get back to work."

He patted my shoulder good-bye and then went out the bridge door.

Before ending my watch on the bridge and rotating back down to CIC, QM3 Edwin came over to my area to grab something. I couldn't tell what she was getting as I tried not to pay attention to her. Walking behind me, she jabbed me with her elbow. When she walked behind me again, she jabbed me once more with her elbow. She didn't say excuse me or anything. By this point, I was ready to punch her in the face.

"Bitch," she said as she passed me.

"You're the bitch," I responded.

"You better stay out of my way," she said.

"No, you better stay out of my way."

At this point, my blood was boiling. I was not about to let her push me around. As she went back to her area, she looked over in my direction a few times, but she never came back. I think she was surprised that I was standing up for myself. Some of the other girls were intimidated by her.

That night, Campbell told me that the next day was going to be a long one. The watch stations would be longer since we were going through the Straits of Hormuz. The water passage there is very narrow and, because it's near Iran, it's important not to cross over into their water. We also had to watch for small boats and dhows, which are small fishing boats, in the water. I told Campbell I would be ready.

The next day, everyone worked hard and took their jobs extra seriously. We began to enter the straits, a passage that would take hours. When it was my turn to rotate up to the bridge, I looked out and could see just how close we were to land. In the distance, I saw two, small speedboats sitting in the water and at least four dhows, all of which had been on my radar.

"Taylor," shouted the CO. "Keep a watch on the surface contacts around here and those speedboats."

"Yes, sir," I answered assertively.

As the Russiantown slowly sailed through the water, a speedboat took off at top speed heading toward the ship. Just as it approached the front of the ship, it turned and headed toward the back. Then a second speedboat headed toward the ship and turned toward the back like the other. They both moved parallel with the ship getting closer and closer.

The CO shouted, "Fire warning shots!"

I felt scared. Walking over to the BM on duty, I asked him who was driving the speedboats. He told me that they were Iranians. The speedboats appeared to be playing a game. Once warning shots were fired, the speedboats rushed off toward the shores of Iran and disappeared into the distance. Our ship wasn't the only one going through the straits. Other naval ships from our combat group traveled with us.

Just as I thought the excitement was over, an alarm sounded and everyone started to run around the bridge. They shouted to put on our Kevlar vests and our helmets. Looking outside the ship, I could see that all of the guns were mounted and looked ready to fire. What was happening? Using my phones, I asked CIC for information. They told me that two Iranian ships with missiles were a couple of miles directly behind us. Looking around, I looked for protection or something I could get under. Then I thought, *Wait a minute. What in the world am I thinking? If a missile hit, I don't think there's any place on the ship where I could go for protection. If a missile hit the bridge, I would be dead.* Standing at the radar, I kept the CO and XO informed as to where the speed-boats were located and how far they were behind us. Little by little, the Iranian ships backed off and turned toward the shores of Iran. I don't know what convinced them to back off, but I was glad that they did. All I could do was stand looking at the radar and take a deep sigh of relief. I hoped that would be the end of the excitement for the day. The rest of the trip through the straits remained quiet, but everyone had their guard up. The stress level was high.

CHAPTER SEVEN

The Gold Souk

The ship pulled into Bahrain on the evening of January 3. Before anyone could go out on liberty, each department had to clean the area of the ship over which they were in charge. Around 1800, those who were not on duty that day were free to go on liberty. After rushing to get ready, I opened the berthing door to find Richards and Farland waiting. I told them to hurry. They gave me a strange look, but I knew that Chief would be looking for me.

Since we didn't have a lot of time as we had to be back at the ship by 2400, we went to the Desert Dome on base to hang out. At the Desert Dome, we could dance to the tunes of a live DJ, play pool, and drink. It was a fun place to hang out, but it was really loud and everyone on the ship went there. The evening went by quickly. The three of us had a good time talking with each other and mingling with different people from the ship. I hung out with a few females from the ship that I hadn't gotten a chance to talk to before. I'd thought they were stuck up, but they turned out to be really nice.

At 2300, Farland and I thought it would be a good idea to get Richards back to the ship. He wasn't falling over drunk, but he had a good bit of alcohol in him. As we waited for the bus to arrive to take us back, more and more drunken people showed up trying to get back to the ship. They weren't all from the Russiantown; some of them were marines or navy from the strike group that travelled with us on deployment.

On the way back, I sat between Richards and Farland. The bus was so loud because of the obnoxious, drunk people. I just wanted to get back to the ship. All of a sudden, a marine who had been sitting in front of me turned around and stared. He was obviously one of the drunken ones. The next thing I knew, he opened his mouth and puked all over the front of my shirt. Already tired and frustrated, I stood up and started to scream at him. The whole bus stopped talking and stared at me. I was so upset that my eyes started to fill with tears. As much as I tried not to start crying, I couldn't help it. Farland didn't know what to say. He kept trying to keep me from crying. Getting off the bus, a marine I recognized as a friend of Williams came over to me.

"You can't go back on ship like that." He began to unbutton his shirt, took it off, and then handed it to me. "Here. Go into that restroom and put this on. I can wear my undershirt on the ship. If I were you, I'd just throw your shirt away."

Taking his shirt, I thanked him. I went into the restroom and came out wearing his shirt. I held my shirt covered in chunks in my hands. He was right. Why keep it? I threw my shirt in the trash. As we all headed up the ship, I told the marine that I would go to berthing, change into my sweats, and come back outside to give him his shirt. He told me he'd be up having a smoke on the smoke deck. After I changed into my sweats, I gave him back his shirt. Still upset from what had happened, I walked over to the railing and just stared at the water beneath me. As I began to cry, Chief came up and leaned against the railing beside me.

"Hey. What's wrong?" he asked. "What happened to you tonight? I was looking for you so that we could go out and get a hotel."

"I went to the Desert Dome with some friends. They'd asked me to go with them. On the way back, some guy on the bus puked on me. I had to throw my shirt away. Some marine from our ship loaned me his shirt."

The next thing I knew, Chief was called down to the quarterdeck.

"I need to talk to you," he said. "Wait for me up here."

As soon as Chief walked down the stairs, Williams came up to me.

"I heard you got puked on," he said.

"What? Did they send out a memo to everyone already?" I said feeling irritated. "Yes, I got puked on. I am so sick of everyone. I wish I could just go home." I thought to myself, *Why do things always happen to me?* I held back tears that were trying to force themselves from my eyes. It wasn't so much that I felt upset or mad; I just felt frustrated. But as soon as I tried to open my mouth to speak, I began sobbing.

"I know what you mean, but you have to just hang in there." Williams sounded very sympathetic.

Williams and I continued our conversation about the incident and he tried to get me to stop crying. As I lifted up my head, I saw Chief out of the corner of my eye. Before I could say anything, Chief appeared upset and turned to go straight downstairs and inside the ship. I could tell that he was jealous that I was talking to Williams. He must have stared at us for several minutes. Williams saw him as well and asked what he was upset about. I told him I didn't know. I told Williams that I'd spoken to Chief earlier and that he said that he'd be back later to talk to me.

"I told you before that he has feelings for me. He doesn't like me talking to other guys on the ship. He gets very jealous. The only reason I'm not saying anything is because I'm trying to wait it out since he'll be leaving soon."

I didn't think that there was anything to worry about because I hadn't done anything. Would Chief write me up for talking to other people on the ship?

As Williams and I prepared to go back inside to go to sleep, Richards and Farland asked if we wanted to go to the mess deck. Before heading down, Williams asked if I'd like to go on liberty with him the following day. I wanted to check out the mosque and he did, too, so I agreed to go out on liberty with him.

When Williams and I entered the mess decks, Richards and Farland were already raiding the food. There wasn't much. Just some apples and oranges. Since I was a little hungry, I grabbed an apple and took it into BFFT. I thought I should check my e-mail again since we were in port. I was afraid that e-mail would go down once we were out to sea. Opening up my account, I had an e-mail from John.

I can't take this anymore! I know what you are doing. I know you've met someone on the ship because you aren't paying any attention to me. I can't sleep, eat, or concentrate. I don't think we're going to work. I'm losing my mind. I think it would be best if we both move on. I'll let you go and do what you want. If you want me to send you anything, let me know because after that, I am done.

His e-mail seemed crazy. I didn't understand what he was talking about. First, he yells at me and accuses me of doing things I'd not done, and then he's telling me that we should move on. Now, he wants to send me a package? Was he out of his mind? I replied to his e-mail.

Why are you being such an asshole? I've been working so hard and working on my officer package instead of sleeping. I already told you that when I'm out to sea, I'm working and don't always have the ability to get on a computer. I don't think you know how much I work on ship. What do you mean move on? You're making me feel as though I'm doing something bad. I think you're the one who's guilty and who's sleeping around. I don't want to read any more nasty e-mails. If you don't have anything nice to say, don't say anything at all. As for receiving packages, I love receiving packages. I don't need anything right now, but just having mail makes my day and reminds me that I will be home soon.

After sending my reply, I made sure to forward the e-mail to my mom. I didn't know what was going on with John, but I thought my mother should keep a folder of his e-mails. I didn't want to keep them on the ship's computer since it was always going down. I logged off, threw away my apple core, and got ready for bed.

That morning, I met Williams to go on liberty. We headed straight for the mosque. Before I could take a tour, I had to dress in the traditional clothing worn by females, which covered everything but my face. When I came out of the back room dressed up, Williams hadn't recognized me. When I went up and asked if he was ready, he jumped back surprised and started laughing. I found the tour very interesting. The building was magnificent, covered in marble and intricately-detailed, beautiful statues. Williams and I spent the day enjoying each other's company, shopping at the mall, and buying gold and other traditional items at the Gold Souq. The souq is a market where one can get good deals on gold and other items such as clothing, shoes, rugs, and purses. It was amazing to be submerged in such culture. I was seeing something that I would have never had a chance to experience had I not joined the navy.

At night, we ate dinner at Chili's and went back to the ship early. The next morning, we had sea and anchor detail. We'd be out to sea for a long time, traveling up and down the waters protecting the oil rigs and undergoing more training.

Since we returned to the ship early, Williams and I decided to go up to the 06 level by the smoke deck to talk. We had really become close friends and were enjoying each other's company. I liked hearing about his family and he liked hearing about mine. While we talked and leaned on the railing, we heard a voice say, "Hey. The smoke deck has been secured." It was BM3 Vargas. I couldn't stand the guy. He reminded me of a pimp. He always eyed women and came across as a wannabe thug. Vargas had beady, little, brown eyes, short, brown hair with a little curl, very tan skin, and a set of teeth that barely fit in his mouth. His teeth were incredibly large with yellow stains. Vargas smoked a lot. The smell of cigarettes spewed out of his pores. When I first checked into the ship, Vargas had asked me out. Of course, I said no. Every time I spoke to him, he seemed to be in trouble. Usually, he was in trouble for stealing. Why they kept him in the navy, I will never know. That night, he was the rover on watch.

"Sorry," Williams responded. "I didn't know it had been secured. We're leaving."

As we began to walk down the stairs to go inside the ship, Vargas yelled, "Before you go inside, can you pick up some of the trash on the deck and throw it away? There are a couple of Coke cans over there," he said, pointing in the distance.

"Sure thing," I said.

With trash in our hands, Williams and I said good night. I took the trash into BFFT, threw it away, and then proceeded into my berthing to go to sleep.

The next morning, I got ready per usual and then went to take my place in CIC for sea and anchor detail. Upon entering, I was told by OS2 Martel that I needed to go to BFFT right away. I would not be participating in sea and anchor detail. That seemed weird. I didn't know why I had to go to BFFT. Smith looked at me, surprised. She shrugged her shoulders and looked as confused as I felt.

Entering BFFT, I saw Chief sitting inside along with Green.

"Sit down, Taylor," Chief said.

OSC informed me that I was being written up for my behavior onboard. I would receive counseling. The news took me by surprise. I had no idea why I was in trouble.

"I found out from a credible source that you were caught making out with a marine on the 07 level the first night on liberty in Bahrain. I heard that you were chased off the deck by three chiefs. I was told to counsel you. You should feel lucky that you're not going to captain's mast. You'll need to sign a counseling chit and that chit will go in your permanent record."

"I don't know what you're talking about," I answered, shocked. "First of all, you can ask Farland and Richards. They were my liberty buddies that night. I was with them all night. When we got back to ship, I went to the smoke deck to return a shirt to a marine. Someone puked on me on the bus and the marine let me borrow his shirt. I spoke with Williams for a short time because I was upset. I saw you come up the stairs, so I know you saw me. We were near the smoke deck. Later, I went to the mess deck with Richards and Farland, and then I went up to my berthing. You said you heard from a credible source? Who is this credible source anyway? I also want to know who the three chiefs were that said they chased me off."

"It was Chief Damage Controlman (DCC) Heidman," Chief answered.

"He is your credible source? Did he say he had to chase me off? Who were the other chiefs?" I asked.

By this point, I could feel my face turning red with anger. I could feel adrenaline running through my veins. I didn't care that he was my chief or that OS1 was there. I intended to stand up for myself. Someone was lying.

"Well," Chief said, "it wasn't three chiefs. It was only DCC."

All of a sudden, his story had changed. How can one accuse someone of something and then suddenly change stories? It felt like a set-up. I felt like Chief was setting me up since I hadn't gotten a hotel room with him in Bahrain. As for Green, she never said a word. She just listened intently. I could tell that she was taking in my story and questioning what Chief said.

"First of all," I said, "I don't even know DCC. I don't even know what he looks like. I've heard his name because I'm supposedly on his fire party, but that's it. He might have thought that he saw me, but it was someone else. How could he even tell who it was? It was so dark outside."

When I asked Chief if DCC had described the female that he saw, Chief said that DCC wasn't sure. He couldn't quite make out who it was, but he just figured that it was me. He said that the woman he saw had dark hair. There was one more point that I had to consider; OSC and DCC were friends.

"That's not all," Chief said. "Last night, BM3 Vargas told me that you and a marine were getting close on the 06 level by the smoke deck. He said it looked as though you two might've been kissing. He said that he told you that the smoke deck was secured and then you both ran inside the ship."

At this point, I knew that I had to stand firm. What was Chief up to? I couldn't let him see me upset. No matter how hurt I felt, I had to show that I could remain tough and disciplined. No one was going to push me around or wrongfully accuse me of something. I looked him straight in the eyes as I spoke.

"I was with Williams. We were outside by the smoke deck talking. We weren't outside long when BM3 Vargas told us that the smoke deck was secured. He asked if we could pick up some trash before going inside. We did what he asked and then we went inside the ship. Neither of us knew that the deck had been secured."

I could feel the heat rising through my body. I felt as though someone had set me on fire. I was reaching my boiling point.

Just then, Green chimed in. "I believe nothing happened, Taylor. People on this ship start talking when they see a male and female together even if nothing is happening. They like to make more out of any situation."

"LT John, who is in charge of the operations department, his junior operations officer, LT Goldburg, CO, and XO also heard of your behavior," Chief chimed in. "LT John is not happy with you at all. He knows that you're going to be sending in your officer package to go to OCS and he thinks that your behavior is unbecoming of an officer. You need to watch your behavior in the future. Now that this counseling session has been completed, sign the counseling chit to acknowledge that we have counseled you."

I felt angry and was reaching the point of wanting to lose control. It took every power in me to keep it together. Nothing that I had to say would get this asshole to listen. He had made up his mind. I could tell by the smug look on his face that he thought he'd won.

Looking at the both of them as though they carried the black plague, I said, "I am not signing the chit. I will not put my signature on anything that is false. I did not do those things. If you want, I am more than willing to go speak in front of the CO and XO, but I am not signing that chit. Take me to captain's mast if you want."

They looked at each other and then looked back at me. They told me that if I did not sign the chit, then I would have to type up a statement regarding my side of the story and why I would not sign the chit. I told them that I would do that and I would have it to them as soon as possible.

I walked out of BFFT and then went inside my berthing. I took a moment to compose myself before going back into CIC. I leaned with my elbows on my rack and my head in my hands asking God why he was making me go through this. I asked him to help me and to make time go by quickly.

Entering CIC, Campbell told me I could help by getting on the DDRT. Smith and Vale, who were on the radar and charts, mouthed, "What happened?" I told them I would tell them later. I knew that I could trust Smith, but I wasn't so sure about Vale. At this point, I didn't even care though. Being on ship was worse than being in high school. News traveled fast. What did it matter who I told? The others probably knew before I even got counseled. How much could one person take?

CHAPTER EIGHT

The Meeting

A fter sea and anchor detail, those not on watch did cleaners in our sections. I always had the same section, which was outside of female berthing and by the female head. Watch sections had been the same since leaving on deployment. New watch sections were finally being assigned. I still had watch with Smith. Flannery and Nicolette were moved into the other section. I didn't mind them anymore. Since they'd gone to captain's mast, they'd settled down and stopped being mean to Smith. They never bothered me. Now Vale and Cameron were in my section. Vale seemed nice, but she was not the kind of person I could trust. I think she liked to gossip. On more than one occasion, she'd shared information with me that someone else had told her not to share with anyone. She could not keep secrets. Cameron was OK, but he could be annoying at times. He thought he was God's gift to women.

As Smith and I swept the floors, Smith asked about what happened during sea and anchor detail. I told her I'd been written up for supposedly making out with a marine on the 07 level. I told her that DCC had spoken with Chief, saying that he thought it was me, but he wasn't sure. Smith couldn't believe it. She told me that she'd always thought Chief was a scum bucket. I told her that I planned to write a statement disputing the charges. She told me that she thought that was a good idea. We talked while we cleaned. Eventually, we heard someone coming down the halls. It was Chief. *Great,* I thought to myself. *What does he want?* We instantly stopped talking. Smith and I finished up our cleaning while Chief just stood in the p-way staring at me. Then Chief asked Smith if he and I could have a moment alone. Smith looked at him for a brief moment and then slowly walked away. She looked back repeatedly to make sure I was OK.

"How are you?" Chief asked me.

"Fine," I said in a blunt manner. I didn't even look up at him. I pretended to be really busy sweeping the p-way. I hoped he would stop talking and walk away.

"You know, I have your back. I know you didn't do those things and I'm here for you," he said softly.

What the heck? Not too long ago, Chief had accused me of kissing marines and showing bad behavior. Then all of a sudden, he tells me that he believes me. Was he mental? There was no other explanation for the way that he was acting.

"I want to talk to you later," he continued. "Tonight. I want everything to be good with us again. I care about you. By the way, how is your officer package coming along? I've been meaning to ask you when you'll be finished." It seemed like a question from out of the blue. Why was he asking me that?

Looking up from sweeping, I said, "Good. It's done. I have all of my recommendations put together. I have one from an admiral plus a few commanders that I worked for when I was a civilian. I just need the CO to read it and then sign his approval."

"If you need anything," Chief said, placing his hand on my shoulder, "don't hesitate to ask."

Once Chief walked away, Smith came over and said she'd heard the whole conversation. She also saw him put his hand on my shoulder. Out of nowhere, Cameron walked over and said that he also saw Chief touch my shoulder and noticed him whispering pretty close to me.

"What did he want?" Cameron asked.

"Nothing. He was talking to me about what happened earlier, during sea and anchor detail," I answered.

After we finished cleaners, Smith and I took off to berthing. Before climbing into my rack, I decided to run down to the drinking fountain, which was on the 04 level by male berthing. Richards was at the drinking fountain.

"Hi," I said.

"Hey. Getting ready for bed?" he asked.

I smiled and said, "Yeah."

Richards suddenly became serious.

"I saw Chief today while you were doing cleaners. He certainly was close to you. I've noticed that he always seems to be around you."

"He's been bothering me and making advances," I said.

"Well, he better keeps his hands off you. If he does anything, you'd better tell someone. Promise me," he said, placing his hand on my shoulder.

I promised him that I would and told him thanks for being concerned. I walked back up to my berthing to get some rest.

That night, I woke up and decided to grab a soda from the machine before going on watch. Vargas was at the machine. If it were possible, I would've shot daggers out of my eyes at him.

"Why did you lie and tell Chief Weinerbangher that I was kissing a marine on the 06 level? You know that wasn't true."

Looking at me and smiling, he said, "Sorry. I wasn't sure. It looked as if you were."

"You knew that we weren't," I said, walking away. Talking to this guy was no use. He was always trying to stir the pot.

Going up the stairs to CIC, I ran into Williams. He asked me to meet him on the smoke deck during mid-rats. He said he had to talk to me about something important. I told him I would meet him there. Williams wasn't a quiet guy, but he seemed quiet and paranoid.

Watch that night passed as usual until around 2000 when LT Goldenrod came looking for me in CIC. She asked Campbell if I could be excused to talk with her for a while. Walking out of CIC, I followed LT Goldenrod to the operations office. Several chiefs, including Chief Lard and Chief Weinerbangher, were inside. LT Goldenrod closed the door quickly and asked if we could go to her berthing. I told her that was fine. Entering her berthing, she sat down across from me. LT John had asked her to talk to me to find out what happened in Bahrain and why I got a counseling chit. The CO and XO also wanted to know the whole story. LT Goldenrod said that it didn't seem like something I would do. As I was about to tell her what happened, there was a knock at the door. Before she could say come in, the door opened. It was Chief Weinerbangher.

"What do you have Taylor in here for? I have already counseled her. It's not necessary for you to talk with her."

LT Goldenrod looked surprised to see Chief.

"LT John wanted me to talk with her," she said, "and to ask her what happened."

Chief looked nervous. He seemed afraid that I would mention his sexual advancements.

"I need to be present," he said. "She will not be doing any talking with you unless I am present."

LT Goldenrod, still looking surprised, told him that was fine.

Once again, I told my story. The LT said that she believed me and would talk to LT John to explain what had happened. She said she would clear everything up. Then LT Goldenrod told me that I was free to go back on watch. As I walked out, Chief followed me. With no one else around, he came up from behind, grabbed my neck, and started to rub it. He leaned into me and told me that everything would be OK. He said that he needed to talk to me later and that he would call for me again to meet him in TACLOG. Chief said that would be the best place for us to have privacy.

During mid-rats that night, I met Williams on the smoke deck. He happened to be the only person there. I felt nervous that Chief might come. I told Williams that I would walk up to the 07 level, wait a bit, and then he could walk up a little after me. Once we were both at the 07 level, he turned to me and spoke.

"I got called into the master gunnery's office. He told me that I'm not allowed to talk to you anymore and that you're a bad influence. He told me that if he heard or saw that I was talking to you, he would send me to another ship."

I was so angry that I could barely respond. I couldn't even swallow given the huge lump in my throat.

"What did you tell him?"

"I told him that nothing happened between us and that you and I were just good friends. I told him that we talk about our kids and our families. He said he didn't believe me and didn't care what I had to say. I would not be allowed talk to you anymore. I guess he must've told some of the other marines, too. They asked me about you and about what was going on."

I told Williams that I was sorry and that I understood. I gained my composure and went back on watch. I didn't know what to think or do anymore. Boy, was I getting screwed over.

Around 0300, Chief got up from his TAO seat on watch and walked over to me on the DDRT. Leaning over me to pretend to look at what I was doing, he lightly placed his left hand on my lower back and slid it down to skim my buttocks, giving them a little tap. He didn't have to say a word. I knew exactly what was on his mind.

"I'm leaving now to go to TACLOG," he whispered in my ear. "I'll call for you in about ten minutes. I'm going to tell them that I need to discuss your officer package with you."

When Chief left the room, I saw Campbell, Smith, Vale, Matthews, and FC2 Theodore look over. Theodore sat in the GLO position where Matthews sat off watch. I didn't talk to Theodore much, but I could tell by the puzzled look on his face that he was curious about what the Chief had said to me.

Ten minutes later on the dot, Chief called CIC and told Campbell to send me to TACLOG. I didn't want to go, but I didn't know what to say. My reputation was on the line. Campbell made a comment about Chief always taking me out of night watch. He told me to tell Chief that I needed to come back right away because of watch stations. Everyone in CIC stared at me as I walked out the door.

Opening the door to TACLOG, I saw Chief sitting in the same chair as always with an empty chair facing him. He told me to sit down. Sitting down, I looked around the room. My heart was pounding. I felt as though I was having a panic attack and all four walls were closing in around me. Grabbing both of my hands, he began to kiss each finger. I tried to pull my hand back, but his hands were twice as large as mine and twice as strong.

"What are we going to tell our spouses? I don't know how I'm going to tell my wife that I'm leaving her for you. Have you thought about what you're going to tell your husband? What will happen when we get back home? My feelings for you are so strong. I don't know if I can hide them much longer. I'm afraid that others on the ship will notice how we feel about each other."

Pulling my hands back onto my lap, I told Chief that I felt uncomfortable and needed to go back on watch. I told him that Campbell needed me for rotation and that I'd been instructed not to be gone for so long. Chief lifted his hand toward me and began to touch my face, stroking his fingers up and down my right cheek. I could feel my cheeks go red hot. I felt nervous and was trying to gather my thoughts together in order to handle the situation carefully.

"I know you have feelings for me," he said. "You're embarrassed to say it. I understand. I'm afraid to get caught, too."

Leaning into me, Chief took both of his hands and placed them around my head. He pulled me forward, his big fat lips puckered to give me a kiss. I leaned my head back and turned my face to the left so that if he kissed anything it would be my ear.

"Stop," I told him.

He stopped for a moment then looked at me and said, "I can't help myself. You know, I know how hard you've been working on your officer package. It would be a shame if you didn't get it."

Again, the chief pulled my face toward him and I felt something wet and slimy on the corner of my mouth. It was his tongue. I closed my eyes and held them tight. All I could envision was his his fat tongue on my skin. I didn't want to see his ugly mug at all. Up and down. Up and down went his tongue. It moved from the top of my lip to the bottom of my lower lip. Backing away, I looked at Chief with disgust and wiped off his spit with the sleeve from my coverall. Everything about him disgusted me. He made me absolutely sick. I had never before felt such hatred and wanted to physically hurt someone until that moment.

I told Chief that I needed to go back to watch, but he told me that he wanted to look at me a while longer. He said that the others wouldn't be looking for me since they thought I was working on my officer package. He just sat and stared at me. It seemed like an eternity. Neither of us spoke. All I could hear was him breathing a heavy breath. It didn't matter if I was on watch or not. It didn't matter what I had to go do. He just wanted to sit and stare at me.

Finally, after a few minutes, Chief told me to get back on watch and to hurry because he didn't want people to start talking. I hurried down the p-way, entered CIC, and resumed my watch station. Campbell stared at me but he didn't say a word. I could tell that he wanted to ask me what was going on. Two hours had passed. I'd spent two hours locked in a room with a pervert. I felt like a caged animal. The rest of watch, I didn't talk to anyone. I couldn't focus on my job. The only thing on my mind was what Chief had just done to me. I became withdrawn.

CHAPTER NINE

The Call Home

The next morning, FC1 Matthews asked me if I'd like to watch a movie later in his office. I told him yes and that doing so sounded like fun. I needed to do something to get my mind off of everything that was happening with OSC. Also, I felt safe when Matthews was around. After getting some sleep and a bite to eat, I knocked on the metal door of ram and found Matthews there. Ram is where the FC's have their office. Ram stands for Rolling Airframe Missle. FC's make preventative and corrective maintenance on equipment as a Guided Missle Weapons Systems Technician.

Matthews handed me a heavy book filled with DVDs and asked me to pick a movie. It felt really good to get away from everyone. As we sat and watched the movie, I kept thinking about going on watch. Was I going to be pulled out again by Chief? There was a loud bang on the ram door. Matthews and I looked at each other. Who would be banging on the door? The other FCs would have just come inside. When Matthews opened the door, we were both shocked to see Chief Weinerbangher standing in the doorway.

"What's going on in here?" Chief asked us.

Matthews looked him straight in the eyes and said, "Nothing. We're just watching a movie."

"Remember, Taylor, you need to watch your behavior on ship. I just came to remind you," Chief said.

How did he even know that I was there? He must have been watching me.

"You know," Chief continued, "FCC Lard and I have been talking about the relationship that you two have. It really needs to be kept off the ship. You don't want to be written up again, do you Taylor?"

"We're just friends," Matthews said. "We don't have a relationship."

"I just came in here to watch a movie," I repeated.

As Chief stood at the door staring at me, he seemed to be waiting for me to leave the room and come with him. When I didn't get up, he slowly turned away and left, closing the door to ram behind him.

Matthews turned to me and asked, "What was that all about? He's never come back here before. He was following you. You know, me and the other FCs have noticed that he always follows you around CIC. He sits next to you and whispers in your ear. What's going on?"

I could no longer maintain my composure.

"He's been coming on to me for months now. He's always pulling me out on watch. He makes me go to TACLOG during watch and then he tries to kiss me and put his hands on me. He always brings up my officer package. I believe he's using it as leverage. I'm just waiting for him to leave. In another month, he's gone."

Matthews sat next to me, reassuring me that he would be there for me. He told me that Chief shouldn't be doing any of that. Matthews made me promise to tell someone if it got worse or if Chief tried anything again. I told him that I would.

Since I didn't have a liberty buddy for our next stop in Bahrain, I asked Williams who he was going with. We both agreed we would go together.

Someone knocked at the door. Matthews thought it might be Chief again. Instead, it was Theodore. He'd come to get some of his snacks to take back on watch. Looking over at both of us, Theodore could tell that Matthews was upset. Matthews asked if he could share with Theodore what was going on. I wasn't sure if Theodore believed the story or not. He just acted surprised. He did mention that Chief was known for giving females special treatment. Theodore walked out of the room and said he'd see us later.

After the movie, it was time for me to go on watch. I felt so uneasy that night. Every time I looked over at Chief, he just stared as though he were pissed off at me. A few hours into watch, Chief got up and left the room. About ten minutes later, a call came into CIC. Campbell picked up the phone. I hoped that I wouldn't hear those dreadful words.

"Taylor," Campbell said putting the phone down. "Go to BFFT."

Damn, I thought. *Here we go again.* Getting up from the radar, I walked down the p-way to BFFT. When I opened the cipher-locked door, I saw Chief sitting in a chair. He told me to shut the door and sit down. I sat down in front of him and he grabbed both of my hands.

"You know, you made me jealous today. You can't be going back there and watching movies with him anymore. Not only do I not like it, but people have been talking. I don't want you to get a bad reputation." He paused for a moment and then continued. "Do you and Matthews have a relationship?"

By this time, I felt frustrated. I knew he could hear it in my voice.

"No, Matthews told you. We are just friends. We do not have a relationship. I am friends with a lot of different people on this ship. Some are male and some are female."

Squeezing my hands, he raised his voice and said, "I don't want you talking to Matthews anymore. Is that understood?"

Who did he think he was? He couldn't tell me who to talk to. Chief leaned forward and tried to kiss me when the door to

BFFT opened. It was Cameron. Boy, did he look surprised to see us.

In a fit of anger, Chief yelled, "Get out!"

In a hurry to leave, Cameron slammed the door. As Chief turned his attention back to me, I felt nervous and shaken by how he had reacted. He continued his speech.

"I want you so bad. All I do is think about you. We have to be together after deployment. I am just worried about how this is going to affect my son. I'm in love with you. Why can't you understand how much you mean to me? Have you thought about what you are going to tell your husband?"

Grabbing my face, he began to caress my cheeks with his thumbs. I grabbed his hands with mine and tried to pull him away from my face. As he leaned in again to try and kiss me, the door to BFFT flew open. Chief quickly moved his hands away from me. This time, Green and Smith stood outside the doorway. They, too, looked shocked to see us in BFFT and to see how closely Chief sat by me. Chief stood up from his chair. His blood was boiling at this point. He grabbed the door and slammed it shut. Thankfully, Smith and Green had not walked in; otherwise, Chief would have hit them with the door. He screamed, "Give me a moment!"

At this point, I felt afraid. The chief's temper and his mannerisms scared the life out me. All I could do was remain still. My body became stiff. Chief told me to get back to watch and not to tell anyone what we'd talked about. Leaving BFFT, I walked passed Green and Smith with my head down. I could feel them staring at me. I didn't turn around to look, but I could feel footsteps following me to CIC. It was Green and Smith. Entering CIC, I saw Cameron sitting by the DDRT table.

Of course, as soon as I got back on watch, Green, Smith, and Cameron wanted to know why I'd been in BFFT. I told them that the chief just wanted to go over my officer package. I gave Smith a telling look with my eyes. I knew by the way that she looked back at me that she understood that the chief was coming on to me again. They stopped questioning me and got back to work.

That night while on watch, I signaled with my hands for Matthews to come over. I told him that Chief Weinerbangher told me not to talk to him anymore. Hearing this, Matthews' lips became tight and his face turned red with anger. The next thing I knew, he walked out of CIC. I wondered where he was going. He was gone for about an hour. When he came back into CIC, he told me that he had taken care of Chief. Matthews had gone to speak to FCC Lard to inform her of what Chief Weinerbangher had said. FCC then spoke with Chief, telling him that it was wrong to tell us not to talk to each other. But being the liar that he was, Chief changed his story and made me and Matthews out to be fools. Chief claimed that he'd never told me not to talk to Matthews. Chief insisted that he'd said only to keep it off the ship. Chief insisted that Matthews and I had a relationship. It didn't matter what I said. Chief was delusional.

For the next couple of days on the ship, things remained quiet. OSC stayed away. I think he felt nervous about doing anything since he'd made such a big scene in BFFT. The ship reached the port in Bahrain. I dressed in civilian clothes, got my bag together, and then went to check my e-mail before meeting Matthews. I had an e-mail from John.

There is no one else, but I know what you're doing. I think we should separate. If you want to date other guys, that's fine. I'm not saying that I am dating anyone or anything. Just make sure that you're being discreet like me.

I replied.

I am tired of getting these e-mails. What is wrong with you? What do you mean I should be discreet like you? It sounds like you're doing something you aren't supposed to. It sounds like you have met someone.

Once I sent the e-mail, I walked out of BFFT. Matthews stood outside of female berthing waiting for me. I told him I was ready to go. Although John's email bothered me, there was nothing I could do about it right now.

We had a fun day together. We ate pizza, went shopping, and spent a little downtime relaxing at an Internet café. We talked a lot about family and different things happening on the ship. We talked a lot about Chief Weinerbangher and his actions. Before making it back to ship, I asked Matthews if I could call home. He told me that was a good idea. He would call home, too, to try to talk to his wife. He didn't know how the conversation would go since they hadn't been getting along. Digging through my backpack, I pulled out a phone card and found an available pay phone. I was so excited to hear their voices.

"Hello?" my mom answered.

"Mom?" I said.

"Lisa, is that you? It's a little hard to hear you."

"Yes," I answered.

"Where are you?" she asked.

"I'm in Bahrain getting ready to go back on the ship."

"How are things going?"

Hesitating, I said, "I...well...I'm having some trouble with my chief on the ship. He's been coming on to me. He's made sexual advances. He follows me around the ship and tries to kiss me. He always talks about my officer package and then tells me to do what he wants because of it. It's like he's using it for leverage. You know that I want to be an officer so badly. He's already gotten me written up for something I didn't do."

Just then, my dad, who was known for listening in on the other telephone, chimed in.

"Did you tell someone on the ship what he's doing?"

"No," I answered starting to cry. The lump in my throat returned. "I don't want to cause any waves and I'm afraid that he'll do something to my officer package. I have it all finished. It was signed by the CO and I'm going to send it from the ship this week."

"He can't be acting like that on the ship," my mom said. "You need to tell someone."

"I'll say something if it gets worse," I said between sniffles.

I told my parents that I had to go. Matthews was waiting for me. Saying good-bye was hard. We said I love you to each other and then I hung up the phone. Looking over at Matthews, I wiped the tears from my eyes and smiled. He rubbed my back to calm my nerves and told me that everything was going to be OK. Matthews said that since we were getting back to the ship early, I could watch one of his movies if I wanted. I told him that sounded like a good idea. I needed something to take my mind off of missing my family.

CHAPTER TEN

Stalking His Prey

The next morning, the ship headed back out to patrol the oil rigs. I couldn't believe it was already the middle of February. Though the ship was scheduled to return to San Diego in June, my mom and Aria would be meeting me in Hawaii to ride the ship back with me to San Diego. They were participating in the Tiger Cruise, which is when family members of those on the ship come aboard. The trip usually takes about two weeks. After sea and anchor detail, a meeting with the OSs was held in CIC. The watch sections would switch times. Since I'd been on nights, I would be on days going forward. I was so happy to hear that because Chief would no longer be able to pull me out of watch.

That morning, a ceremony would be held on the flight deck to welcome the new CO. His name was CDR Moorehouse. He'd already been on the ship for a couple of weeks. I'd passed him once in the p-way. He seemed nice, but he walked around fist-pumping at everyone. I guess he thought he was cool. I was glad that I didn't have to go to the ceremony as I'd be on watch.

I really enjoyed watch during the day. It passed by quickly, which surprised me. I felt relieved knowing that Chief wouldn't have watch with me so he would never pull me out. Besides, he would be at the ceremony. At 1700, after getting off of watch, I took a quick nap and then went into BFFT to get my officer package ready to mail. It took me about an hour to get all of my materials together. While I was finishing up, the door to BFFT opened. Chief Weinerbangher and Chief Lard entered. Chief Lard glared at me, camel toe and all. She didn't look very happy.

"Taylor, what are you doing in here?" she said. "Are you the only one in here?"

Surprised, I said, "Yes, I'm working on my officer package."

They both left, the door closing behind them. I looked back at the computer. *I wonder what that was all about*, I thought to myself. Five minutes later, the door opened again. This time, Matthews walked in. He looked pissed off. He slammed the door and then sat down next to me.

"Guess what?" he said.

"What?" I answered.

"Chief Weinerbangher came into the operations office while Chief Lard was there. He told Chief Lard that you were in ram with me. He said that you and I were having a relationship on the ship. Chief Lard told him that he couldn't possibly have seen that. Chief Weinerbangher looked puzzled and asked why. She looked over at me sitting at the computer and told him that I'd been doing work for her for hours. Then Chief Lard asked me if I knew where you were. I told her that you were probably in BFFT working on your package."

When Matthews told me this, I was not surprised. This wasn't the first time Chief had tried to get me into trouble. I kept thinking to myself, *Only a few more weeks until he leaves the ship.*

A few days passed and I began to prefer watch at night versus during the day. Day watch was so busy; a lot seemed to be going on. The ship did most of its training and drills during the day. The only thing that I didn't like about night watch was that Chief had watch then. That's when he'd pull me out to talk to him because it was dark on the ship and most people were asleep. I couldn't wait for the next day. Chief Weinerbangher's replacement would be coming on. I'd only have to put up with Chief for a few more weeks. Hopefully, he'd be busy training the new chief to take over.

The new chief's name was Chief Tartlette. He looked half Caucasian and half African American. He was a small man and very slender. He wasn't bad looking even though he was completely bald. Chief Tartlette's head was so shiny that it made me want to rub it with my hand to see if it made squeaky noises. The new chief appeared to take good care of himself as he looked physically fit.

The day had arrived when I was finally going to mail my officer package. I was so excited. I felt certain that I would get picked to go to OCS. I made sure that my package was outstanding. The CO and XO had both looked it over. I had top test scores plus several letters of recommendation including one from an admiral. At the post office, I handed my package to SSgt Williams as he worked there. Williams looked so happy for me as he told me that my package was in good hands. I made sure to send it return receipt with signature confirmation.

That night, I went to the gym before going to bed. I knew that would be a good time to go because the gym was fairly empty at night. Having changed into my PT uniform, I grabbed my towel and headed down to the gym. When I got there, there was only one other person there, a guy on the treadmill. I knew that I'd seen him on ship before, but I didn't know who he was. Putting my towel on the stair-climber, I began my workout.

After about fifteen minutes, the gym door opened and there stood Chief Weinerbangher. He looked at me and then looked at the guy on the treadmill. He slowly shut the door but never came in. I wondered what he was up to. Five minutes later, the gym door opened again. It was Chief. He looked at me, again looked at the guy on the treadmill, and then walked out. Another twenty minutes later, Chief Weinerbangher opened the door again and then walked in. As soon as Chief walked inside, the guy on the treadmill stopped and ran out of the room. Chief just looked at me and then got on the treadmill. Feeling uneasy and nervous,

I stopped my workout and gathered my towel. I didn't want to talk to him. As soon as he noticed that I was preparing to leave, he stopped the treadmill and walked toward me.

"I want you right now," he said, placing his arms around me.

I told him that I didn't think that was a good idea and I really just wanted to work out.

"I want to kiss you," he insisted, puckering up his lips.

When I took a step to walk out the door, Chief blocked me with his ogre-like body. Leaning into me, he grabbed my shoulders and held me tight. Just then, the gym door flew open. It was the guy that had been on the treadmill. He'd forgotten his towel. Chief jumped back in a panic. The guy looked at us and then walked out. Chief looked as though he'd just seen a ghost.

"Do you think he saw us? I better leave. This wasn't a good idea."

He left the room in a hurry. I followed behind and went straight to berthing. At that moment, I wished that I could tell Smith what had happened, but she was sound asleep. I couldn't go anywhere on the ship. It felt like no place was safe.

After putting my sweats on for bed, I decided to go down to the soda machine to get something to drink. I felt so thirsty. Opening the berthing door with caution, I looked around and then stepped out into the p-way. I hurried to the soda machine. Opening my soda, I walked down the p-way when I heard someone calling my name. It was Chief. I swear he seemed to know what I was doing at all hours of the day. It was almost as though he'd put a tracer on me.

"I have to see you tonight. "I have to talk to you. I can't control myself anymore." He had a crazy look in his eyes. It was a look of lust. He acted as though he was going out of his mind. He started shaking and said, "I should not have tried that in the gym. I hope that guy didn't see anything. We need a place where we can just be together. Please meet me tonight."

"I can't," I told him. I looked him straight in the eyes and said, "I have to go to sleep."

At that moment, Richards walked by. He was on his way to the bridge to go back on watch. As he passed, he looked at Chief and then at me. Chief looked as though he would tell Richards to hurry up and keep walking. Before Richards went up the stairs to the bridge, he turned back and looked at me. I looked back. Even though he didn't say anything, Richards seemed to know that something was going on. Earlier that day, I'd seen Richards on the mess deck. He said that he'd noticed Chief lurking around a couple of times when I was doing cleaners. I told him that I was still having problems with the chief on ship and that he continued to make sexual advances. I wondered if others on the ship had noticed anything and if they said anything about it. One thing I did not want was a bad reputation. Walking away, I could feel Richards staring at me.

That night, I had a hard time sleeping. The night seemed to last forever. In the middle of the night, I got up to go to the bathroom. Crawling back into my rack, I lay there thinking about home and how uncomfortable the racks really were. I had little space to move around and the blue, privacy curtain made me feel claustrophobic at times. With my eyes open, I could see a slight light coming from the doorway. Someone had come into berthing. I assumed it was one of the girls on watch getting something from their rack. The footsteps appeared to be moving toward my rack. The footsteps were heavy. As they got closer, I could hear deep, heavy breathing. The only person I knew who breathed that deeply and heavily was Chief Weinerbangher. Frozen in fear, I saw a large silhouette appear outside my rack. The person stood, staring and breathing down on me. I don't know how long the figure remained. All I knew was that it seemed like an eternity. Slowly, the figure turned and I heard footsteps walking away. The door opened and then closed. Even though I didn't see him, I knew in my heart that it was Chief Weinerbangher. What I couldn't figure out was how he knew which rack was mine. It was so dark in the berthing and there were so many racks.

I didn't get much sleep that night. I woke up early and went on watch. McGraw must have been happy. She was the person I'd relieved on duty. During watch, I confided in Smith what had happened the previous night. She told me that I should've woken her up. I told her that by that time, the chief would've been gone anyway.

In the middle of watch, OS1 Green told me that it was my turn to clean the head. I hated cleaning the head. The females were always so dirty. Gobs of hair got stuck in the shower drain and the toilets were always clogged up. Walking out of CIC, Green told me that Vale was already in the head and would help me.

Walking down the p-way, I was surprised when the TACLOG door suddenly opened. It was Chief. I swear. How did he know that I was going to be walking down the p-way at that very moment?

"Taylor, wait," he said in a soft voice. "I need to talk to you."

I pretended not to hear him and walked straight into the head. I figured that he couldn't walk in there. He wasn't allowed. I grabbed my cleaning gear and stepped into one of the stalls. The head door opened and Chief barged in. He walked over to the stall where I was cleaning and told me that he had to talk to me. I couldn't believe my eyes. He was standing in the female head. Vale stepped out from the shower area.

"Chief?" she said.

"Vale," he said, startled. "I didn't know you were in here."

Chief ran out of the head in a hurry. Vale just stood in the middle of the room and looked surprised.

"What's going on? A bunch of people have been talking about you and him. They know he has a crush on you."

Looking at her, I didn't know what to say. I didn't trust Vale, but I felt like I needed to get things off my chest. Besides, I didn't want her to think that I was having a relationship with Chief. I told her everything that had happened. She told me that I should tell someone, but I told her that I only had a couple of weeks and then he would be gone. I could stick it out until then—couldn't I?

CHAPTER ELEVEN

Incident

The USS Russiantown began to have engine problems and required an emergency stop in Bahrain before heading back home. I tried to avoid Chief as much as I could. This was my time to enjoy myself off ship and to do some last-minute shopping for Aria. I couldn't believe we were heading home soon. It seemed like a dream. Once sea and anchor detail was set and the ship left Bahrain, the watch stations switched again. I was back on night watch. Campbell was in charge of watch again. I liked Campbell. Even though he always seemed like he hated life and had a dry sense of humor, he was nice to me and left me alone to do my job. If I had questions, he would take the time to show me what to do and to answer my questions. I couldn't compare Weissman and Martel to him. I hadn't worked with Weissman. She did her own thing. Martel mainly worked during the day and he didn't talk to many people. Martel didn't care for his job anymore since he would be getting out of the navy soon. He didn't have a bad attitude; he just had a short-timer's attitude.

Green only had watch during the day. She didn't like having watch at night. I don't know why; she just didn't. I liked Green, but at times, she could be a little intimidating. She had a certain way of doing things and she liked everyone to follow her way.

That night, I started watch on the bridge. I felt calm knowing that I would be up there a few hours before going into CIC. I wondered if Chief was on watch and if he was waiting for me to come down. After rotating, I went down to CIC to take my place on the DDRT. Sure enough, Chief was on watch and kept turning around to stare at me. A couple of times, he even got out of his seat and leaned over the DDRT table to talk to me about my time in Bahrain. He told me that he was planning to leave watch to go to TACLOG. He would call for me there. First of all, Chief sure was gutsy talking to me in front of everyone. Second, I wondered what Chief planned to tell my watch section this time.

Early morning hours came and Chief got up from his watch section seat and walked out of CIC. About half an hour passed and then a call came into CIC. I had a feeling it was Chief calling for me. Sure enough. Campbell looked at me.

"Taylor," Campbell spoke. "Chief wants to talk to you again in TACLOG. Why does he always pull you out during watch? You end up being gone for an hour or more. We need you in here."

"I don't know," I said, shrugging my shoulders. "He didn't say why I needed to go there?"

"I need you here," Campbell answered. "Didn't you already mail your officer package?"

"Yes," I said.

Campbell told me to go see what Chief wanted, but to tell him that I needed to come back to watch. I knew that was easier said than done. I'd told Chief that before and he didn't seem to care. No one would go against his word. Chief was in charge of all of the OSs. Besides, he had all of his chief friends — a good ole boys club — who would cover for him or stick up for him if needed.

As I entered TACLOG, Chief stood in the middle of the room looking at me. He wasn't in his chair like usual. He told me to close the door and then he took my hand. He wanted me to follow him to another room in the back. The rooms were divided by a cipher lock. The other room was half the size of the first with one chair in the corner. I could also see a lot of items from the marines on ship. On the floor was a big, green, wooden box, which looked as though it could hold quite a lot of marine gear. After he shut the door, he squeezed my left hand tight and smiled.

"Stand on the box."

I froze. I wondered if he sensed my fear. I didn't want him to see that I felt intimidated by him.

"I said stand on the box," Chief repeated. "I want to look at you."

I didn't say a word. I didn't know if I should stand on the box or just do nothing. Grabbing my other hand and squeezing it, the chief used a more forceful voice.

"Stand on the box!"

The box was several feet high. Since the chief had both of my hands in his, I had a hard time getting on top of the box. I used my leg muscles to push myself up.

Staring at me, the chief said, "Let me look at you. I've been thinking about this all day. I want you sexually. I've been wanting to sleep with you since Bahrain. I had everything all planned there, but you never waited for me to go on liberty. I know you want me. You can't hide your feelings."

Grabbing my face with both of his hands, the chief began to lean forward like he was going to kiss me. I tensed my body and tried to lean away from him. Feeling his grip tighten, I could tell that he was not happy. As his face got close to mine, I tried to shut my eyes. I didn't want to see him. I told him to stop.

Just before he made contact, I opened my eyes and saw his big, long, slimy tongue come out of his mouth. With a slow and steady stroke, he placed his tongue on my cheek and started licking me like a dog. I felt his saliva on my face and smelled the reek of cigarettes. Before I knew it, my face was engulfed in saliva as he kept licking my cheeks, jaw, and lips. It was the most disgusting thing I'd ever been through. It made me feel sick. By this point, I couldn't stop shaking. I remained frozen in fear and felt short of breath.

Still holding my head, he leaned away from me and stared. Moving his hands off my face he said, "I want to feel inside you." He stopped looking into my eyes and began studying my chest. He grabbed the zipper on my coveralls and began pulling it down until it reach my waist area barely revealing my belly button. He placed both of his hands upon my breasts and began to squeeze them as though they were balls of Silly Putty. I pushed his hands away.

"No," I told him.

In response, he grabbed hold of me tighter. Pushing him away seemed to anger him. He held me so tight that it hurt my arms. I felt as though my life flashed before my eyes. I wished I could freeze time and get away. Before I could move, he placed his hands under my white shirt and then ran them down to the elastic of my underwear. Just as he was about to slide his hands down, he looked at the cipher door for a brief moment, letting down his guard. Thinking fast, I kneed him in the groin and pushed him out of my way. I opened the door to the room and took off running down the p-way to CIC. While I ran, I zipped up the zipper to my coveralls. Since it was night, there wasn't anyone in the p-way. Most were sleeping or already on watch.

When I entered CIC, I was out of breath and my eyes began to tear up. Everyone looked at me, but no one said a word. Smith knew that there was something very wrong.

"What happened?" Smith asked. "What did he do? I know something happened. I can tell from your face."

Quietly, I told her. I didn't want everyone else to hear.

"You need to report this when we get off from watch," she told me. "If you don't report it, then I will."

I felt scared. So scared. Why was this happening to me?

CHAPTER TWELVE

Secret's Out

As Smith and I continued to talk in berthing, Vale came in and asked what had happened. She agreed with Smith that I needed to tell someone. Smith told me to stay with Vale in berthing while she went to CIC to tell Green that she needed to talk privately in BFFT. She said it was an emergency. Green followed Smith right away. A few minutes later, Green came into berthing and told me to come with her into BFFT. She wanted to talk. With Smith in the room for support, I told Green everything that had happened between Chief Weinerbangher and me. I wanted to hold back my tears, but I couldn't. Green looked as though she'd seen a ghost. Her skin went pale and she looked as though she were about to cry. Green told me that she had to report the incident to the command; she had no choice. Green told me to stay in berthing until further notice.

When Smith walked me back into berthing, a couple of the girls whose racks were next to mine came up and asked what happened. I knew them somewhat and had spoken to them before, but I'd never hung out with them. Even so, they'd always been very nice to me. CT2 Miller had very long brown hair. I'd always thought she was very pretty. She looked very feminine, small and petite. The other was CT2 Mayor. Mayor was blond and very tan. Every time I'd seen her on ship, she was in a good mood. Sitting down with both of them on the berthing floor, I began to tell them what had happened starting from the beginning.

"That pig," Mayor said. "The man has always been a pig. He likes to use his size to intimidate women. You know, I had a run-in with him last deployment and had him written up."

I was surprised to hear this. I asked her what happened.

"Well, last deployment he started making advances at me," Mayor proceeded to tell me. "When I didn't respond, he had me written up. He said that I was talking too much with the marines on the ship. He tried to give me a counseling chit. I refused to sign it and went straight down to CMC Weiss and filed a report. Someone talked to Weinerbangher and told him to leave me alone. Ever since then, he's taken a dislike to me, but he leaves me alone."

As we talked about Chief, Green came in and told me that CMC Weiss has been informed of the situation by Chief Tartlette. Green told me that I would be called down to CMC Weiss's office to meet with him and the Equal Employment Opportunity (EEO) representative to put in a statement. The new CO, CDR Moorehouse, and XO LCDR Dennis would also be notified.

Chief Weinerbangher entered BFFT and asked Green and Smith what was wrong. Before Green would speak to Chief, she said that she was going to get Chief Lard to sit in. Green walked over to the operations office and asked Chief Lard if she would please come into BFFT. When Chief Lard and Green entered the room, Smith shut the door.

"What is this all about? I heard it has something to do with Taylor. Is she mad because I accused her of having a relationship with FC1 Matthews?" he asked, looking bewildered.

Green began to cry. "I trusted you. How could you do this? Taylor told me what happened. Did you make sexual advances toward her?"

Chief Lard looked at him and asked, "Tell me you didn't do this. Were you alone with her in a room?"

Putting his head down, Chief said quietly, "I have done some things in my life that I am not proud of."

"You know better than that," said Chief Lard.

"She wanted this relationship as much as I did. I told her that I was afraid to get caught and that we needed to watch ourselves. That's why I was stopping it," Chief responded.

Between the tears, Green told Chief Weinerbangher that she had already informed the command of what he'd done. Unable to control her tears, Green left BFFT and came into berthing with Smith. Before she could sit down and talk with me, CMC Weiss and the EEO representative knocked on the door and said that they need me to come down to CMC's office to give a statement.

Picking myself up off the floor, I followed them to the office. I sat in a chair facing them. I gave my statement starting from the beginning when Chief made the comment about me belly dancing and called me attractive. I told them how he called me out of watch for hours and then pawed me with his hands and tried to kiss me. I mentioned every instance I could think of in my statement. I gave names of witnesses as well. The EEO representative told me that LTJG Oleander was the legal officer assigned to the case and she would get with me shortly.

Walking out of the office, I headed back to berthing hoping that I wouldn't run into Chief. Little did I know that Chief was on his way down to the CMC's office so that they could get his statement. I knew in my heart that the man would lie or somehow put everything on me so that it appeared to be my fault. I wish I could be present to hear what he would say. The only information I received of what happened in the office came from Oleander. She wanted me to know what was going on.

"As Chief Weinerbangher entered CMC's office with his friend, Chief Bohger, Chief kept his head held low," Oleander said.

"Sit down," Weiss said. "You understand that what you've done is unbecoming of a naval chief and you should have known better. The EEO officer has taken Taylor's statement and now we're going to take yours."

Looking up with anger in his eyes, Chief said, "Let me see her statement. What did she say?"

"I'm sorry, but you are not allowed to see her statement," Weiss answered. "This is the time for you to make your statement regarding what happened."

Chief began. "I have to admit that I may have done some things that were not right. I stopped before it went too far. Taylor and I had a relationship that she condoned. She started getting upset with me when I had to counsel her for having relationships with marines on the ship. She also became upset when I questioned her about having a relationship with FC1 Matthews and I told her to keep it off the ship." He paused for a moment. "Before I say more, I would like to be issued an advocate. I would like Chief Bohger to be my advocate."

"That's fine," said Weiss. "You are free to go, but you are no longer allowed in CIC, the ops office, or BFFT. This is by order of the Commanding Officer. You are also to stay away from Taylor. You are to have no contact with her. Also, there will be no talking to anyone about this issue. I will inform you of what happens next."

The room filled with silence as Chief Weinerbangher and Chief Bohger left the room. Chief Weinerbangher went to the chiefs' mess. Chief Bohger returned to work.

After spending a few hours in berthing, Green came and asked me if I was OK to go on watch. I told her yes and then followed her to CIC. As soon as I entered CIC and assumed watch on the radar, LTJG Oleander stopped in to CIC and asked if she could talk to me for a few moments. Leaving CIC, I followed Oleander into her berthing.

"Go ahead and have a seat," she said. First of all, I want to know whether you will be making this a formal complaint or an informal complaint."

Looking at her puzzled, I asked, "Well, what's the difference?"

"A formal complaint goes out in a message navy-wide to let everyone know of the situation. An informal complaint stays within the ship."

Knowing that I would catch a lot of heat for doing this, I told her that I was filing a formal complaint. Why should I keep what this monster had done within the ship? I wanted the world to know what he'd done and I wanted to be a role model to other women going through the same thing. What he did was wrong and he should therefore be punished.

Oleander continued, "Please, start from the beginning. Try not to leave out any details and if you have any witnesses, it would be helpful to give me those names. This process may take a while. I have a lot of people to meet with and a lot of information to gather."

With that, I began my story. I made sure not to leave out any details. I told Oleander about leaving watch and being stuck in BFFT, the ops office, and TACLOG with Chief. I described how he forced me to kiss him and how he would hold my face and lick my mouth and cheeks with his slimy tongue. I told her how he followed me around the ship and always brought up my officer package. What I thought would only last a few moments turned out to last an hour. Once I was finished, I left Oleander's office and went back on watch. Although I knew deep down in my soul that I had done the right thing, I couldn't help but feel that maybe I should have just kept things to myself. Everyone on watch kept staring at me. I felt so uncomfortable and even a little sick to my stomach. I wished that they would stop looking at me, studying me with their eyes. It felt as if they were talking to me without opening their mouths to say anything. I could hear it now: *I wonder if she did anything with him? What did he do to her? Were they having a relationship?*

Later that evening, Chief Weinerbangher was requested in CMC Weiss's office. Weiss informed him that I requested a formal complaint be made and that the complaint had been filed. The corresponding situation report was also being released. This meant that a message was being sent to the entire naval community. Weiss handed Chief papers to review and sign; he would be provided with a copy. Before Chief could leave the office, the EEO officer came in and handed Chief the navy's EEO program instruction. Chief Weiss told Weinerbangher that he was free to go, but he would receive word as to when captain's mast would take place. It wouldn't be any time too soon since LTJG Oleander would be investing the case and supplying them with her findings.

Once Chief left the office, he headed straight down to medical. People who had seen him walking through the ship said he seemed quiet and kept his head down. Entering medical, he met with Senior Chief Knight.

"I...I need to talk...about a health issue I'm having," Chief Weinerbangher said in a pathetic voice.

"Well, let me know how I can help you," responded Senior Chief Knight. "Can you wait one moment? I'm going to go get something from my desk."

As Knight stepped out of the medical office, Chief Weinerbangher sat in a chair with his head down and his hands clasped in his lap.

"Ok, sorry about that," Senior Chief Knight said, returning. "Go on and tell me what's happening."

"I'm having suicidal thoughts," Chief told the doctor.

Senior Chief Knight looked concerned and asked Chief to talk to him about why he was having such thoughts.

"I'm just feeling as though I don't want to live anymore. I just recently started to have these thoughts. I didn't know who to talk to."

After talking for forty-five minutes, Senior Chief Knight told Chief Weinerbangher that he would be right back to continue their conversation. He had to take care of something. When Senior Chief Knight returned, Chief Weinerbangher stood up and took back his previous comments.

"I feel much better now and my thoughts of suicide are gone," Chief Weinerbangher said, jumping to his feet and walking out of the medical office.

Senior Chief Knight was confused beyond belief. One moment, he'd been talking to someone ready to commit suicide and the next moment, that same person stands up in a hurry and says he's fine. Senior Chief Knight sat feeling confused.

Chief Weinerbangher sat in his berthing thinking about what he'd just told Senior Chief Knight. Images of what he'd done to a fellow sailor raced through his head. Although the chief had denied what he'd done, his conscience was getting the better of him. As I stood watch on the radar, thoughts of what others thought of me and what my future entailed weighed on my shoulders.

CHAPTER THIRTEEN

Investigation

LTJG Oleander began the investigation into the sexual harassment charge filed against Chief Weinerbangher. I knew it would be a very long process and that many individuals would be interviewed. I also knew there would be those who took his side, especially the other chiefs since they all stuck together. Further, when Chief made advances, most of the time he'd done so behind closed doors to keep others from seeing what happened. Luckily, he made a few slip-ups, such as whispering in my ear during combat, keeping me from watch, and following me around the ship staying as close to me as possible.

LTJG Oleander reached for her pencil and pad of paper to take notes.

Statement of OS3 Smith: "Taylor confided in me what was happening to her. I witnessed Chief always staring at her in CIC while on watch and he would call to have her taken out of CIC. She would be gone anywhere from one to two hours. Taylor told me how he made sexual advances toward her. The reason Taylor took so long to file an EEO complaint is that Chief Weinerbangher constantly used her officer package as leverage. She was also afraid that people would view her as a bad person who caused drama."

Statement of OSSN Nicholas: "Well, on the morning of February 17, I heard through OS3 Vale that Chief was accused of sexual harassment by Taylor. I was shocked. I never would have thought of Chief sexually harassing someone. I never observed anything inappropriate. Right now I am unsure that Taylor is telling the truth."

Statement of OS2 Kowlesky: "Chief often showed favoritism to females. It became more noticeable about eighteen to twenty-four months ago when there were fewer females in the OS division. He'd be nicer to females than to males and gave females stronger evaluations."

Statement of CMC Weiss: "I remember one time when Chief Weinerbangher came to my office. He seemed a little distraught about a female sailor, OS2 Agnes. OS2 Agnes was on the ship about a year ago. Sitting down in front of my desk, he held his head down and started mumbling something about her. When I asked him what was wrong, he told me that he had feelings for Agnes. He said that he needed to 'step back' or words to that effect."

Statement of CT2 Miller: "During the USS Russiantown's last deployment, I wrote a statement about Chief Weinerbangher. He'd written me up on a counseling chit stating that I was being overly friendly to marines on the ship. I was pissed. It was a total lie. I wrote a statement against his accusations and said that he was being unprofessional. He would get jealous when the females talked to other males. I went down to CMC Weiss's office on more than one occasion because of Chief's behavior, the way he was treating me. Chief tried to show me special attention and when I wouldn't pay attention to him, he would get angry. He's a very unprofessional person and his leadership style is inconsistent. It amazes me how this man thinks. He sets standards for everyone else, but he doesn't follow the rules himself. He would muster the whole OI division, telling us that food was not allowed in CIC during watch and that no one should be falling asleep. Then he turns around and brings food into CIC for himself during TAO watch. He falls asleep all the time in his chair. He's pathetic."

Statement of OS2 Campbell: "Several months ago, I had a conversation with Chief. I told him that I didn't think he was doing his job well. I also told him that I didn't like the fact that he showed favoritism towards females over the males. Chief even admitted to me that he showed favoritism toward females. He really favored OS2 Agnes. She was his favorite. I thought it was weird when Chief would pull Taylor out of watch for hours at a time. It's not typical for anyone to do so. I had an idea that something might be happening, but I wasn't sure."

Statement of BM3 Vargas: "So, I saw Taylor talking with some marine near the smoke deck in Bahrain and told Chief Weinerbangher. I know I said they were kissing, but I really couldn't tell for sure; they just looked close. I told them that the deck was secured and they left and went inside the ship. Do I think Chief is capable of sexual harassment? Yes, I do."

Statement of OS1 Green: "I was upset to hear that Chief could have done anything like this. I trusted him and now that trust is gone. Deep down, I suspected something was going on. One time I tried to enter BFFT and was surprised to see Chief there sitting close to Taylor. They were alone in the office. He got mad and shut the door in my face and told me to give him a moment. I found it unusual that he was alone behind a closed door with her. I also wondered why he got so upset by my entering the office."

Statement of OS3 McGraw: "I have never known Chief to act inappropriately. I never witnessed anything between him and Taylor."

Statement of OSSN Richards: "Taylor told me what Chief Weinerbangher was doing to her. I told her that she needed to tell someone. I know she was afraid to tell anyone because he was using her officer package as leverage. What he did was disgusting. One time, I happened to see him staring at her during cleaners. He was always following her around the ship. Another time, on my way to watch on the bridge, I saw him standing really close to her in the p-way. When I walked by, he just stared at me and I stared back. I could tell something was happening by the look on Taylor's face. She looked at me as though she felt afraid but couldn't say anything. Her body looked stiff and she leaned away from him. I wanted to ask if she was alright, but I didn't because he's a chief. He probably would have told me to go back to watch and mind my own business. I know Taylor was really upset that first night in Bahrain when he'd written her up because DCC said he saw her making out with a marine. That was I lie. I was with her on the mess decks and then I saw her go into her berthing. I never saw her on the deck of the ships at all after she went into her berthing."

Statement of SSgt Williams: "I first met Taylor a couple of months into deployment. I would talk to her out on the 06 level. We have a lot in common and talk about our kids and work. We're friends and that's it. As we were talking one day, Taylor confided in me and told me that her chief was bothering her and coming on to her sexually. I urged her to tell someone, but she said that she didn't want to cause any problems and that he'd be leaving anyway. After Taylor mentioned the issue, I started to become aware of Chief Weinerbangher staring at her whenever he passed by. He also looked angry at me when I was talking to her. Taylor and I did go on liberty together in Saipan and Bahrain, but we just hung out as friends. In Saipan, we went to a dance club where her chief was. She'd gone to get some drinks and I saw her talking to her chief. When she came back, she looked upset and told me that he'd told her to ditch me to go get a room with him. She said he was probably just drunk, but I have to admit I was pissed off. I told her I was going to go tell him something, but she wouldn't let me. After Bahrain, I was told by my command to stay away from Taylor and not to talk to her since they thought Taylor and I had been on the 07 level making out. Neither one of us went up there. I saw Taylor go into her berthing as I headed down to mine."

Statement of OS3 Vale: "I didn't know anything was going on until OS3 Smith made a comment about OSC always looking at Taylor and whispering to her. After I started paying attention, I noticed how he favored her, but I didn't think anything of it because I knew that OSC favored girls over boys. But then one day I was cleaning the head and happened to be in the shower. I heard a male voice yell Taylor's name in the bathroom. When I stepped out, I saw Chief standing in the middle of the head trying to talk to Taylor. As soon as he noticed me, he got scared and backed out of the bathroom fast. Taylor looked upset and so I asked her what was going on. She told me that for months, Chief had been coming on to her and that he'd pull her out of watch and force her to kiss him. I told her that she needed to tell someone. She didn't want to. I told her that he needed to stop and if he made more advances toward her that she had to tell someone."

Statement of FC1 Matthews: "Chief is a pig. I've seen him standing over her in watch, rubbing up against her, whispering in her ear, and following her around the ship. He's jealous whenever she talks to a guy. On a couple of occasions, he's tried to get both of us into trouble saying that we're having a relationship on the ship. He told her not to talk to me. Taylor and I are friends. He followed her one time into ram because I'd asked Taylor if she wanted to see a movie. She told me that she needed to take her mind off of Chief because he was making her feel so uncomfortable with all the sexual advances. Sure enough, he comes pounding on my door looking for her. He wanted her to leave ram, but she told him she was only watching a movie. When she didn't leave, he walked away upset. That's when he talked to her about staying away from me, claiming that people were talking about us having a relationship."

Statement of Senior Chief Knight: "I wasn't aware of any sexual harassment going on between Taylor and Chief Weinerbangher. This is the first I've heard of anything. Chief Weinerbangher came down to medical to discuss some health issues, but he never mentioned Taylor."

CHAPTER FOURTEEN

Spreading Rumors

Sitting on the ship, I didn't know who I could trust. I couldn't go anywhere to get away. I was surrounded by water. My family was miles away and my husband had become the biggest jerk in the world. By that point, everyone on the ship knew what had happened. CMC Weiss informed me that CDR Moorhouse and LCDR Dennis were going to set up captain's mast for OSC. While we were both on the ship, there was to be no mention of the case to anyone. I knew right away that not mentioning the case would be easier said than done. Others were already talking about it nonstop. OSC must have been discussing it with the other chiefs on ship since they were friends and helped each other out. I was told that OSC was not allowed in BFFT or CIC. He'd been removed from his watch.

That afternoon on my way down to the mess decks, I was walking down the p-way when a couple of male sailors passed by and acted like they were coughing. They both stared at me and then said, "Slut." I looked back at them as they started to laugh. I felt so small inside. It made me doubt myself and made me wonder if maybe I had done something wrong. Maybe I was a slut. I quickly stopped myself from thinking such things. I had to remember that it wasn't me; it was OSC. It took all of the strength inside me to continue down the p-way and stand in line for dinner.

All eyes were on me. I could feel it and I could see people whispering to one another and then looking in my direction. A couple of times, I heard people whisper words like slut and whore. I wanted to yell at them to stop, to leave me alone, but I knew that I had to keep it together. I didn't want to give anyone the satisfaction of seeing me upset. Something was said about me. OSC must have said something. He would do anything to defend his actions. After I ate, I went to BFFT to get on the computer before going on watch. I decided to send John and my parents an e-mail explaining what was going on. John must have been on the computer because I got an e-mail back right away.

I don't know what to tell you. You probably wanted it anyway. I'm done.

One would think that a spouse would be supportive. My spouse should be the person I go to when I need help. I guess that wasn't the case. I didn't respond. I had nothing to say. It was useless to try and talk with him.

That night on watch, Vale came up to me and Smith. She whispered, "I heard Chief talking about you and the case to people on the smoke deck today. He was telling them how you'd gotten mad at him because he caught you with different guys. He was telling them about the relationship he'd been having with you. He called you a slut and whore. He said that you sleep around and was telling some of the sailors on ship about the incident where you were caught making out with marines at night on the ship. I know it is not true, but most of the people on the ship don't. He was also asking different people to come forward for him and to speak for him at captain's mast. He was telling people that you're a liar. He came up to me and asked me to speak for him. Originally, I told him that I would, but I'm not going to now because I know he did those things. I told him I would because I was afraid to go against his orders."

"What a jerk," said Smith.

I looked at both of them and said, "He's not even supposed to be discussing the case. Thank you for telling me, Vale."

Vale went to her watch station and I proceeded to talk to Smith.

"I can't believe him. Today people were staring at me and calling me slut and whore."

"I know what you mean," Smith looked down and continued. "Some BMs came up to me and called you a slut talking about your relationship with OSC. I stopped them and told them that they didn't know the whole story. I told them that OSC was starting rumors and lies to save his ass. They stopped and listened to me. No one said a word after that."

"Thank you for doing that," I told her.

Life didn't get any easier for me. People still called me slut, whore, and hooker behind my back. No one wanted to be around me anymore. I only had a few friends that stuck by my side, in particular Smith and Matthews. They remained my best friends on the ship. If it hadn't been for them, I would have lost my mind.

After watch, I went to BFFT to check my e-mail. There was another e-mail from John.

Lisa – You still aren't showing me affection after I've asked for it. You never call, and when you do, you want to talk to your parents. I AM DONE! I AM DONE WITH YOU! I don't know what to say anymore. You are too busy for me. Besides, I know what you're doing on the ship. I won't come out and say it, but I know you're seeing someone. That's fine because I've met someone.

What the hell did that mean? I felt so confused and pissed off. My neck became hot and my jaw tightened. What did he mean before when he mentioned being discreet like him? I responded.

John – How dare you send me that e-mail. I never get to use the phones on the ship because I'm always on watch. I have told you that I'm dealing with a lot right now because of my chief. The e-mail always goes down, so I never get to send as many e-mails as I would like. When I'm in port, I do call, but you never answer your phone or you're not there. I can't talk for a long time either because it costs me a lot. Also, I'm using a phone card and I'm trying to make it last. I'm not doing anything on ship. I can't help it if you can't deal with my being gone.

Why was this happening to me? I had everything going on with OSC and my husband continued to send me nasty, mean e-mails. It was apparent that he was having an affair. It felt like my whole world was crashing down on me.

Getting ready for bed, I felt sick to my stomach. I just knew deep down that John was sleeping around. At that point, I couldn't worry about him. I had to worry about the situation I was in on ship. What was going to happen at captain's mast?

CHAPTER FIFTEEN

Captain's Mast

L eaning against the wall outside of the chiefs' mess, I felt my stomach churning. I'd be called in soon to speak in front of CDR Moorehouse, LCDR Dennis, CMC Weiss, and Chief Bohger. I could hear a lot of yelling and occasionally heard Chief Weinerbangher's voice. Within a few minutes, the yelling stopped and Chief Bohger opened the door. He told me to come inside. Looking around the room, I didn't see OSC. LCDR Dennis told me that OSC would not be present. He'd gone to another room. LCDR Dennis told me to start from the beginning. They wanted to hear the whole story.

As I talked, flashbacks danced through my mind. I felt as though I was reliving it all over again. I didn't even notice if the others were looking at me. When I finished speaking, I stood in front of them as they stared back at me. They told me that I was free to leave. I was asked to send in Vale who was standing outside. When I opened the door, I saw Vale and told her that they wanted her inside. She entered and closed the door behind her.

Walking to berthing, I opened the door and sat next to my rack on the floor. I thought about the situation and realized that turning Chief in was the best thing I could have done. I knew that he'd bothered other women before. I wondered how many he'd slept with or raped. I couldn't let it happen again. I had to be the one to stop it.

As I sat quietly, the door to the berthing flew open. It was Vale and she was crying.

"What happened?" I asked, picking myself up off the floor.

Trying to talk, she couldn't quite get all the words out. Her face looked red and blotchy as tears streamed down her face.

"Chief...," she hesitated for a moment. "Chief came at me."

Puzzled, I asked, "What do you mean he came at you?"

"They brought him into the room while I was describing what I'd seen. I told them how he was in the female berthing and then yesterday—I didn't tell you—he came up to me and told me that I had to promise to speak for him and that I better not say anything against him. All of a sudden, he called me a liar and told me to shut up. Then he came at me and put his hands on around my neck. Chief Bohger and CMC Weiss jumped up and grabbed him. Then LCDR Dennis and CDR Moorehouse got up and tried to help settle him down. Everyone was yelling. I didn't even know what was happening, it all happened so fast."

"Are you serious?" I asked.

I couldn't believe it. OSC had lost it.

I had no idea how the rest of captain's mast went. It wasn't until later that evening on watch when LTJG Oleander came into CIC and asked if she could speak to me. As we stood in the p-way, she told me that the CO and XO had found OSC guilty. He would be leaving the ship the next day by helicopter. He'd be put on a flight back to the states from Bahrain.

Before I could open the door to go back into CIC, OSC Tartlette came out to find me. I hadn't spoken to him much since he was so new.

"Taylor, everything alright?" he asked.

"Yes, everything is fine," I answered and went back on watch.

CHAPTER SIXTEEN

On My Way

After OSC left, the ship seemed much quieter. I knew that I still had to watch my steps very carefully, though, because of Chief Weinerbangher's friends. They were always watching me, trying to get me into trouble any chance that they could. We'd just reached Guam, which was our port before Hawaii. Once we got to Hawaii, I'd get to see my mom and Aria who'd both be flying out for the Tiger Cruise. On the cruise, they'd be able to participate in special events that take place on the ship. For instance, the Russiantown would have movie, karaoke, and game nights. During the day, they'd be able to tour the ship and look at the different marine equipment.

While most of the sailors got off the ship for liberty, I had to stay on because my section was on watch. I didn't mind. I didn't want to get off the ship. I was just happy to finally be going home. Before anyone could leave for the day, all sailors had to muster on the flight deck for a speech from the CO. It was the first speech I'd been to given by the CO on the ship. I was usually on watch. The

CO went on and on about liberty behavior and how great we were all doing. He also told us that it had come to his attention that sailors were misusing the word *shipmate*. Instead, they were saying *shitmate*. He wanted to change the word *shipmate* to *sea warrior* and asked that we refer to our fellow sailors as sea warriors. Looking around at the other sailors in the group, I noticed that some were laughing at him. I heard them say that sea warrior sounded stupid; shipmate had been around forever. The CO was something else. He ended his speech by putting his right fist in the air and said, "Fist pump!" He asked that whenever we passed him on the ship, he wanted a fist pump. *What the hell is that crap?* I thought to myself. *Fist pump?* I guess that was supposed to motivate us.

Taking a break on the 06 level, I decided to call home. My cell phone worked well in Guam. I decided to give John a call on his cell phone. The first call I made rang and rang without going to voice mail. It was as if his phone had been shut off. I tried a second time and the same thing happened. So, I called home.

My dad answered. "Hello?"

"Hi, Dad. Where's John? I tried his cell phone but it's shut off."

"Well, he hasn't been home all week," my dad exclaimed. "He packed up a bag, said he was helping a buddy move, and that he wouldn't be home for a week."

That was strange. I grilled my dad more.

"Do you know what buddy it was and where he was going?"

"I don't know," my dad said. "He didn't say anything to anyone. He hasn't called either."

I felt that sickening feeling coming over me again. It made my gut hurt. I just had a feeling that something was still wrong.

"Dad, something is wrong. I know it. I know he's sleeping around. Can you please go to the bank and pull out the money that I have saved up? I don't trust him. He's on my account."

"Sure, I will do that," my dad said quietly.

I didn't feel like talking much, so I told my dad that I would call again later because I had to get back to work. The whole day, all I could think about was where John had gone and who he was with. I remembered my mom telling me that she'd noticed his things slowly disappearing from the bedroom and that he was gone a lot.

Sitting
Looking at the water
Reflections
One drop of water, streaming down
Creating a ripple in the water
For only my abadoned heart to see
Alone

While on watch that night I could help but think about everything that was happening in my life. It was easy to think, since I was on the bridge radar and there was not a contact in site. A contact is any ship, boat, land mass, or object that appears on the radar. The only sailors on the bridge besides myself were a BM steering the ship, QM navigating, Operation Officer and Chief Tartlette. Thinking to myself; *where is Chief Tartlette anyway? I thought he was suppose to be up here.* It was hard to see because it was so dark. As I turned around behind me, there was a stack of large metal boxes. On top of the boxes I saw a large figure of a body that appeared to be laying on its side with some kind of material over it. As I stepped closer, I noticed that it was Chief Tartlette. He was asleep on watch with his jacket over his torso. With a light tap of my fingers, he began to move. I couldn't see his face clearly, but I knew he had just woke up from the grogginess of his voice. As he stood up, he put his jacket on without saying a word and walked up to the front of the bridge to stand next to the operations officer.

I thought, *What just happened? Was he seriously just sleeping on watch?*

This story was too good to keep to myself. As soon as I went down to CIC after rotation, I had to tell everyone that I found Chief sleeping on the job.

CHAPTER SEVENTEEN

Tiger Cruise

Pulling into Hawaii, I felt so excited. Aria and my mom would not arrive until the following day, but Williams and I had made plans to get off the ship and spend the day together shopping. I still thought about John a lot, but I couldn't dwell on him as I knew there was nothing that I could do about it. Besides, I'd tried calling him as soon as we docked and still there was no answer.

During the day, Williams and I walked all around town and went into different kinds of shops. He was always looking at things for his son and, of course, I was always looking for Aria. I knew that she arrived the next day, so I figured that she and my mom would want to do some shopping. As the evening set in, my feet were tired. Williams was hungry and asked if I wanted to get a bite before going back to the ship. I told him that sounded good. We found a small, beachside restaurant where we ate burgers and drank margaritas. We watched the sun go down one sip at a time. It was great. I felt so relaxed. We had fun talking about people on the ship and discussing our childhoods. That night, for the first time ever, I couldn't wait to get back to the ship to go to sleep. I was going to see my mom and Aria.

The next morning, I got ready and headed into town. I'd checked out with Williams, but he was going to the beach with the guys while I met my mom. We'd decided to meet up later that night to check back into the ship. My mom had told me that she'd meet me at the hotel where she'd rented a room. We'd just be using the room to rest for the day. Entering the hotel, I spotted them in line right away. They were checking in. As I ran up to both of them, I started to cry and gave them a big hug. My mom explained to the man behind the desk that I'd been on deployment and that they were meeting me to ride the ship back. After saying hello and wiping away our tears, we rested in the room before going shopping and getting a bite to eat. Once again, I told my mom the whole story about Chief Weinerbangher. She still couldn't believe it. She told me that my dad was furious.

After we ate, I gave Williams a call to find out where we should meet. He said he'd meet me at 2200 where the taxi drivers drop people off before walking down to the ship. I told him that was fine. I figured he would be drunk since he spent the day out with the guys, but he wasn't. When we met at 2200, I introduced him to Aria and to my mom. He introduced them to his friends as we walked toward the ship. Walking onto the ship, Aria looked around and was amazed at how big it was. After checking in my mom and Aria, I told Williams I'd see him the next day.

When my mom and Aria entered female berthing with me, all the girls came up to Aria asking her name and age. She acted very shy, but she told them her name and that she was nine years old. Miller and Mayor took Aria by the hand and told her that they had a special bed just for her. She would be in a middle rack. They put a soft blanket there for her. My mom's rack was in the middle as well, right across from me. The first thing my mom asked was, "How do I get up into the bed?" I told my mom to put her foot on the lower rack, watch her head, and then jump up. Of course, it didn't work. She still couldn't get up. So I told her to face the rack and step up on the bottom rack. Then I told her to put her chest on the rack and extend her arms out like Superman. From this position, I was able to grab my mom's legs and push her into the rack. I wish I'd had a camera. It was so funny. Some of the other girls laughed.

Before going to sleep, OS1 Green came into the berthing to let me know that since I had family on board, I would be off watch the whole way to San Diego. I would get to enjoy myself. I couldn't believe it. That was the best news. I could spend the whole time showing my family around the ship.

The trip back to San Diego was fun. Aria had a good time playing games with some of the marines on the ship. Williams made her popcorn and got her soda. My mom didn't enjoy the trip so much. She hated going outside because of the cold wind and she didn't like being surrounded by water. She also hated the fact that she couldn't get a cup of coffee on the ship. I told her that wasn't unusual for the USS Russiantown. Of course, if you were an officer then you had access to coffee, ice cream, and good, fresh food, but if you were enlisted, forget it. The morning before we were to port in San Diego, the sea warriors were required to meet with their families on the flight deck to listen to a speech by the CO. He let everyone know what time we'd be getting sea and anchor detail. Of course, the CO ended his speech with a fist pump.

The morning we pulled in, OS1 Green informed me that sea and anchor would be at 1100. I would not be in CIC. Green said that she needed me dressed in my whites in order to man the rails. She said that my mom and daughter could stand behind me and watch the ship pull in. Getting dressed in my whites, I made sure that I looked perfect. I couldn't wait to see my dad and grandma, who would both be down on the pier. I knew that John would be down there, too, but I didn't want to see him. I knew that the only reason he would come was to see Aria. He could've cared less about seeing me.

Manning the rails, I looked out to San Diego. I'd never noticed how beautiful it is. I couldn't have asked for a more perfect day. The sky looked bright blue as there wasn't a cloud to be seen. The sun felt warm as it hit my face. The closer the ship got to the dock,

I slowly started to distinguish family members who were waving and yelling. Many people held up signs and carried flowers to give to their loved ones.

I scanned the crowd up and down looking for my grandma. Much to my dismay, the first person I saw was John standing with his arms crossed looking straight ahead. No smile, no waving, nothing. Next to him stood my dad and grandma who were both smiling and waving. Once the ship came to a complete stop and anchored, I was told to muster in CIC before leaving on liberty. Once I got the go-ahead, my mom, Aria, and I exited the ship. I grabbed what I wanted to take with me and went ashore. My dad and grandma gave me a huge hug. John remained cold. He showed no love at all. I think he wished that I had stayed out to sea. He didn't look at me or talk to me. He gave Aria a small hug and that was it. I don't even know why he came after what he'd told me in his e-mails. On the way home, I really wanted to ride in the car with my parents, but I ended up riding home with John. Not one word was spoken. Every time I said something, he completely ignored me.

Thinking back, I remembered when John had gone on deployment. He'd gone on four since we'd been married. Every time he came home, I'd greet him with open arms. Once I even flew his mother out from Indiana to see him come in. I knew that would be something he'd like. I felt proud of him for serving our country and for doing what he did. I guess he couldn't be proud of me.

CHAPTER EIGHTEEN

Unanswered Questions

It was my first Sunday morning waking up at home. I'd planned to go to church with my parents and Aria, and then to eat breakfast. As I left for church, I thought about calling John to see if he planned to meet us at breakfast. I was in such a hurry that I left the house and forgot to ask him. He had never been one to go to church; anything involving free food, on the other hand, and he would be there. Of course, the only reason that breakfast was free was because my dad paid. John never offered to contribute. He was very selfish when it came to his money; he kept it for himself. John and I hadn't spoken about the e-mails he'd sent me while I was on deployment. It seemed like he didn't want to talk about anything. Maybe it was because of the other person he'd met. When I finally did call, I could tell that John had just woken up. His voice sounded very groggy.

"Yeah?" he said.

"Hey," I said in a cheery voice. "Are you meeting us for breakfast?"

"Nope," he answered.

I was surprised. I didn't know why he'd answered no so quickly.

"No?" I asked him. "You're not going to breakfast?"

Without hesitation, he answered, "Nope. I want a divorce and I'm moving out today. I'm bored with you. Besides, you're too independent and I don't like that."

"What?"

"Yeah, I've been thinking about this for a while. There's no one else or anything. I mean, I'm not leaving you because I'm interested in someone else. I just don't want to be married to you anymore. I think a divorce would be best."

As he spoke, I was in disbelief. I couldn't breathe and barely got any words out.

"Do you want to go to counseling? I don't want a divorce. How is this going to affect Aria? What am I going to tell her?"

"I'll talk with Aria," he answered. "She'll understand and she'll be fine. I don't want counseling. I just want a divorce."

"I know you met someone else. You told me before in the e-mail. I thought we could fix things or work on our relationship. Are you sure you want a divorce?" I asked again.

"Yep," he said. He paused for a moment and then continued, "Wait—well, I was thinking about going to breakfast first because I'm hungry. I can meet you after church. When I get home, I'll pack my things and go."

What in the world was I hearing? Did I seriously hear him correctly? He's going to leave me, but he needs to go to breakfast first so he'll have the strength to come home and pack his bags. Hell no. What an idiot.

"Don't bother!" I yelled. "How dare you. Pack your shit and get out of the house now. What—you need to fill your stomach and get energy to come home and leave me and your child? You are an asshole."

After our conversation, my blood boiled. I broke out in a sweat. I felt so mad that I couldn't even cry. I knew it. I just knew that there was something going on. I felt pretty sure that another woman was in the picture. *Eleven years of marriage and four deployments and this is what I get?* I thought to myself. *This man is the biggest asshole that ever walked the face of the earth.* What was I going to tell Aria? Going to church and breakfast was hard that day. I told my parents what happened. Aria asked me if her daddy was coming back. Looking her in the eyes, I cried and told her that her daddy would not be living with us anymore. She never cried; she just looked at me with her green eyes. When we got home from breakfast, John was gone. Most of his things were gone as well except for some marine awards and certificates and photo albums.

As Aria looked around our bedroom, she leaned over and picked something up from the floor by the desk. She was so quiet. What was she looking at? Walking over, I noticed that she was holding a bunch of her school pictures. She held out her hands to me and said, "I found these in the trash." Her eyes looked like they were filled with a wet gloss. Her face looked flush; her cheeks were light pink. The pictures had been in his wallet. For some unknown reason, he'd thrown them away. He never bothered to talk to Aria to tell her why he was leaving. He gave no explanation. I began to cry, took the pictures from Aria, and hugged her.

The next day was a work day so I had to go back down to the ship. There wasn't much to do besides clean up CIC by putting away charts. It surprised me that I'd not heard back regarding my officer package. I'd sent it months ago and I knew that the board had already met thanks to a naval message that I'd read. I'd also heard from other officers on ship that the board usually met in the spring. It was June and I'd not yet heard anything. I'd received the signed return receipt from my package, so I knew they'd received it. I thought that maybe I'd better call. I wanted to go so badly. That was what I'd worked for. After tracking down the number online, I called. A man answered the phone.

"Hello," I said. "My name is OS3 Taylor. I'm on the USS Russiantown. I submitted my package for OCS in January and was wondering about the outcome of my package. I've not seen any names come out on a naval message."

"Hold on," he said, putting me on hold. "No Taylor here. I don't have any record of your package. We never received it."

"Wait — how can that be? I have the receipt in my hand signed by a person saying that they received my package. It couldn't be lost."

The man became rude, talking over me. "We don't have it. It's lost. The board already met. You will have to wait until next year."

By now, I felt frustrated. There was nothing more I could say to this man. When I asked to speak with someone else, he told me that there was no one else to talk to. After getting off the phone, I intended to find out what had happened to my package.

I requested a meeting with CDR Moorehouse to let him know that my package had been lost. I thought that maybe he could contact the proper people and fix things. As I entered his office, CDR Moorehouse told me to sit down.

"So, Taylor, what can I do for you?" He sat straight up in his chair with his head held high as if to let me know that he was above me. He looked down at me as he spoke.

"Sir, my officer package has been lost. I called OCS and the man in charge of the packages there said that they never received it and that it must have gotten lost. That can't be possible. I have the receipt that they signed." I looked at CDR Moorehouse right in the eyes as I spoke. I wanted him to know that I was serious.

He shifted his weight in his chair and folded his hands on his desk. "Taylor, these things happen. You can always apply again next year. I don't know what to tell you. I'll try calling again and will let you know what they say."

I agreed, but it seemed as though he was just appeasing me and could actually care less. This was my third time applying to OCS and my application was now lost. Over the next couple of days, I talked to LCDR Dennis and to OSC Tartlette. I also told some of the other officers on the ship. They couldn't believe what had happened. CDR Moorehouse never got back to me. No one would give me any answers. One day as I was sweeping the p-ways, the supply officer poked his head out of his office and told me that he wanted to speak to me. He told me to come into his office and have a seat.

"Taylor," he spoke very softly and then shut the door. "Don't say anything, but your officer package was not lost. Someone pulled it. I thought you should know. You better get back to sweeping the p-ways."

Standing outside his office, I couldn't understand what I'd just been told. So my package was not lost and someone had it. Who had it? Who could have pulled it? The only one with enough power to pull my officer package would be the CO. I assumed that he'd had my package pulled because of the situation with Chief Weinerbangher. What was I going to do? Was there anything I could do?

CHAPTER NINETEEN

Appeal

Still wondering about what had happened to my officer package, I spent my weekends on watch. It wasn't too bad because Smith was in my watch section. While in berthing, I heard over the intercom that the watch section needed to report to the mess decks. I picked myself up off the floor. I really didn't want to go down there. I knew that they would make us clean or take out trash. Sure enough, I had to collect trash from CIC, BFFT, and the operations office. After I gathered all the trash together, I started down the ladder wells outside the ship and stopped in to see Smith. She was petty officer of the watch, which meant that she gave all of the announcements for the day and rang the bell when needed. She also carried a nine millimeter handgun. That was my favorite watch.

When I stopped in to talk with her, Smith told me to look out by the ship. Looking overboard, I spotted OSC talking to one of the BM chiefs. I had to go down to take the trash off, so I was going to have to pass him. What was he doing there? According to the CO, he wasn't allowed on or near the Russiantown at all. Smith seemed surprised to see him as well. Walking off the ship with the trash bags in my hand, I could feel him staring at me. I didn't even look. I walked directly to the trash can. He wasn't about to do anything anyway because too many people were around. As I headed back up to the 06 level of the ship, different people came up to me asking why he was there. I told them that I didn't know. Just as I entered berthing, I got a text message from Smith. She told me that OSC was on the ship headed up to the 06 level. Right away, I hurried out of the berthing and down the p-way. LTJG Oleander was in my watch section. I knocked on her door. She told me to enter.

"Ma'am, Chief Weinerbangher is on the ship. I saw him when I went down to take out the trash. He was staring at me. He isn't supposed to be on the ship."

She looked up from her paperwork and appeared surprised. "No, he isn't supposed to be here. Do you know where he went?"

"No, ma'am," I answered.

LTJG Oleander got up from her paperwork. She told me to stay in her room. She would be right back.

About fifteen minutes must have passed before she returned and told me that Chief was off the ship. She told me that he knew he was not supposed to be on the ship, but the BM chief had signed him in thinking everything was OK as long as they stayed together. Before I left LTJG Oleander's room, she told me to sit back down. She had something that she needed to talk to me about.

"Taylor, Chief filed an appeal and is taking the case to trial before a board. We're going to have to get witnesses together to see if anyone will come forward for your case against him. It's going to be hard. The board will question you extensively. Be prepared for the worst. Just tell your story and don't let them intimidate you."

The closer the trial date came, the harder LTJG Oleander worked to get witnesses together. The day before the trial, she came to see me and told me that luck was on my side. A group of women would be coming forward to tell their stories about

OSC. The first person would be CT2 Miller. She'd told me before that he'd made advances toward her when she first came on the ship. When she didn't respond to his advances, he'd made it difficult for her. He was always looking to get her into trouble and he'd even written her up on her last deployment saying that she'd been overly friendly with the marines on the ship. Gee, that sounded familiar. BM3 Breyers would be the second witness. A lot of people on the ship thought that she was a slut. I always liked her and never thought she acted inappropriately. I think a lot of the other women were jealous because she was attractive and the guys seemed to like her. She was very tall with long, blond hair. She was a little chubby, but she had a pretty face. She'd always been very nice to me. She'd had run-ins with Chief Weinerbangher during which he went into the female head unannounced and even looked under the bathroom stall that she was in. BM3 Breyers also caught him going into female berthing unannounced. The third female that came forward was a sailor who used to be on the ship. LTJG Oleander interviewed her by teleconference. No one would tell me much about her; all I knew was that she'd been removed from the ship due to inappropriate behavior with Chief Weinerbangher. I couldn't believe the number of women that were stepping forward to help my case. It was clear that this man was a pervert. I felt proud to be fighting for what was right, not only as a woman, but as a person.

The trial took place on base in the same building where the admiral worked. Chief Weinerbangher had been working in that building since being removed from the ship. I felt nervous standing outside with the other women. LTJG Oleander informed us that we'd be going in one at a time. Chief Weinerbangher would be there. LTJG Oleander informed us to let him get the best of us and not to let him intimidate us.

Within a few minutes, the door opened and I was called in first. Entering the room, I noticed Chief sitting in the front on the left. He just stared at me with a smug smile on his face. He watched my every step as I walked across the room to sit in a chair positioned by the board table. At the table sat four officers: two CDRs and two LCDRs. None of them showed any expression.

They looked at me for a brief moment and then looked straight ahead. Perhaps they were looking at LTJG Oleander since she would be making the opening statement for the trial. As I looked around the room, I noticed a woman sitting on a bench behind Chief. She looked Asian with medium-length, brown hair and a very round face. She looked plain in that she wasn't wearing any makeup. As she leaned toward Chief, I saw her stare at me with a mean look on her face. I gathered that she must have been his wife. LTJG Oleander stood and began.

"This is the case of OS3 Taylor accusing Chief Weinerbangher of sexual harassment on ship." Turning to look at me, she continued. "Taylor, I want you to tell the board the series of events that took place up until reporting this incident."

I began my story.

"I'd been on the ship a couple of months before Chief started making sexual advances. I didn't think anything badly of it at first. I thought that maybe I was overreacting. The first time he said anything to me, I was on the 06 level when he came over to me. I told him that I missed my family. He informed me that he had a son that he also missed. We started talking about our kids since they were about the same age. I proceeded to tell him how much I liked to dance and that I'd taught dance before joining the navy. I told him that I knew many styles including belly dancing. He told me that he thought I'd look good in a belly-dancing outfit and that he'd like to see that sometime. He told me that I was an attractive woman. I felt uncomfortable when he said that, but I let it go.

"Things got worse on the ship. He removed me from watch on different occasions and I'd be gone anywhere from minutes to hours. He'd call the watch area and tell the CO on watch that I needed to come to BFFT, TACLOG, or the ops office so that he could talk to me about my officer package. When I went to see him, he'd shut the door, put his hands on me — my face, my neck, or my hands — and then he'd force me to kiss him. He told me that he was falling for me and had feelings for me. He told me that he was going to leave his wife for me. I told him that what he was doing was inappropriate, but he told me that he couldn't help his feelings and that he knew that I felt the same way. I was afraid to say anything because I was new to the command and I didn't want to make waves.

"On one occasion, he had written me up for making out with a marine on ship on the 07 level, which was untrue. At first, he was all for punishing me. I refused to sign the chit because it was not true. I told him to take me to captain's mast if he needed to or to let me talk to the CO. I was being falsely accused. Initially, he told me that he had three credible sources that saw me making out. The next thing I know, his story changed and he told me that only DCC Heisal said he'd seen me. That was the only person. I wrote a statement disputing the charges and spoke to LT Goldenrod. Chief walked in on our conversation stating that he wanted to be present. After speaking with her, Chief changed his story once again. He told me that he believed me. He said he was on my side.

"Life on the ship became unbearable. He began following me around. He'd follow me everywhere: outside, ram, gym, and even into the female head."

As I continued my story, the room stayed silent. I wished that the whole trial would just be over. I continued to tell the board about the last incident in which I was trapped in TACLOG. I felt embarrassed telling them the details about him fondling my breasts and putting his hands down my unzipped coveralls. As I told my story, no one in the room moved. Everyone sat still, looked at me, and listened, including Chief and his wife. When I finished, I looked at LTJG Oleander. She nodded, signaling that I was OK and that I'd done a good job.

Hearing a man clear his throat, I looked over at the board of men sitting at the table. The man in the middle, a CDR, looked at me and asked gruffly, "So what makes you think that you didn't egg on the situation? You didn't come forward right away. Why come forward now?"

My face became rigid. My mouth tightened, I held my head high, and I looked him straight in the eyes.

"I was new to the command. I was new to the navy. I was out to sea in the middle of the ocean wondering how I was going to handle the situation. I didn't want to cause any problems because I knew that it would hurt my career. The one thing I wanted the most was to make OCS and become an officer. The reason I'm here today is to protect all of the young girls that come into the navy and might meet up with this man." I pointed to Chief. "No girl or woman deserves to be treated with such disrespect. I understand that this has happened before, but it's going to end with me."

I continued to look right into the CDR's eyes. The whole board remained silent for a while. One could've heard a pin drop. LTJG Oleander looked at me and then told me I was free to step out of the room. I could return to the ship. I was told to send CT2 Mayor into the room.

I'd never felt so stressed in all my life. Walking back to the ship, I couldn't help but rub my neck and my head. I had the worst headache. My neck felt stiff and tight. It hurt just to move my neck from left to right. I hoped that the other women were OK while giving their own statements. As soon as they came back on the ship, I would be sure to give them a huge thank you. I owed them so much for stepping forward and telling their story. I realized that it took a lot of courage to do so since their reputation was on the line. I would never forget that.

That afternoon, my phone rang. It was John. I didn't want to talk to him. Just the sound of his voice made me want to vomit.

"Hey," he said. "Have you filed for divorce yet? You need to hurry up and do that."

Wait a second. This man asked me for a divorce, left me and his child, and wanted me to do the paperwork to file for divorce?

"John, you're the one that wants a divorce. You file the paperwork."

"You file it. I'm not going to. You said you were going to do it anyway. I want you to hurry up," he said impatiently.

I couldn't handle him. I figured I shouldn't need to. There was no reasoning with John. I knew he had another woman. That was probably why he wanted to hurry up with the divorce.

"John, I will file the papers when I file them. I don't know what else to tell you. I'm done talking to you." Those were the last words out of my mouth before I hung up on him.

After that conversation, John harassed me for a few weeks until I filed for divorce. I must have had at least thirty text messages every day telling me to watch my back or else. He'd call and hang up all day long. I guess the man had nothing else to do with his life. Funny thing was, like I said before, he left me. Why would he call and harass me when he was the one who wanted to go? Ultimately, I was letting him go. His harassment eventually ended with the help of my lawyer who threatened to file a restraining order against him. That shut him up for good.

Shortly after, John posted pictures of his new motorcycle online. He said it was a divorce present he'd purchased. He also posted pictures of his new girlfriend, Suzanne. I don't know what he saw in her. She was the ugliest woman I'd ever seen. Her skin looked like she'd been baking in the sun for years. She had platinum-blond, straight hair that fell to just below her shoulders. She had a very strong jaw line, which made her look like a man. Looking at the picture of her, I paid close attention to see if she had an Adam's apple. I really couldn't tell. In one of the pictures, she was smiling, which showed all of the wrinkles on her face. Aria looked through some of the pictures and saw some of them at SeaWorld and in Las Vegas. Aria looked puzzled.

"Mom, when did you go into the navy?

"Why?" I asked.

"Well, these pictures date back to 2007."

"Yeah," I answered. "I'd just left for deployment."

Now didn't that show John's intelligence. Why would he post pictures online for the whole world to see and then put a date on them? What an idiot. Hopefully his family would see the pictures and the dates and then put two and two together. They hadn't spoken to me since John left. One day, his parents came to see Aria. I tried to talk with them, but they wouldn't even answer me. They gave me the cold shoulder. I knew he'd told them another one of his lies to cover up his affair with another woman.

CHAPTER TWENTY

Help? What Help?

Every single day I wondered what had really happened to my officer package. I thought about the fact that the supply officer told me it had been pulled and that someone had it. As for Chief Weinerbangher, I never heard anything about the trial or what happened. I knew he was still attached to the USS Russiantown, but he was working in the admiral's building. He must not have been kicked out or he would've had to check out on the ship.

One day while on duty, I couldn't stop thinking about how much I wanted to become an officer. It wasn't fair or right that my package got pulled because some fat, nasty chief decided to sexually harass me. Who could I contact? The command wouldn't help me. Calling OCS was useless. I wondered if Naval Criminal Investigative Service (NCIS) could help and could investigate what had happened to my package. I wondered if they could look into whether or not it got pulled, and if it did, then who pulled it and why. So, that's what I did.

After getting their number, I called NCIS and a man answered the phone. I told him my name and why I was calling. He didn't give me the time of day. He told me that he couldn't help and that they didn't handle cases like mine. I told him the whole story of what happened to me on ship and he still told me that they couldn't handle the case. He was very quick to get me off the phone. I think the real reason that they didn't want to help me was because they didn't want to take a case that involved the navy. It was a case that they wanted to keep swept under the rug.

After I got off the phone with NCIS, I called my mom to tell her what had happened. My mom told me that I should think about contacting my congressman and put in a congressional. I needed answers as to why the OCS board signed the receipt stating they received my officer package and now all of a sudden they are saying they never got it. It has vanished. What a good idea. I hadn't thought about that. I decided that the best congressman to contact would be Congressman Stewart. He'd been in the military himself and he seemed to be supportive of our military. Once I got off the phone with my mom, I dialed information to get his number. When information connected me to his office, a recording came on and I left a message. I gave them a brief explanation as to why I was calling and left my number hoping that someone would call me back. Taking this approach would make even more waves. The issue wasn't just about my package; it was about the chief as well. Why didn't he ever receive any punishment? Why didn't anyone on the ship let me know what was going on? I felt left in the dark.

A few hours after leaving the message, my phone rang. I didn't recognize the number as it looked to be from out of town.

"Hello?"

A man with a very deep voice said, "May I speak to Taylor?'

"This is Taylor."

"My name is Wayne. I'm calling for Congressman Stewart. He's in Washington, DC, at the moment, but we got the message you left and are willing to look into your case. Could you start from the beginning and tell me what happened?"

I couldn't believe it. Someone was actually going to help me. Finally, I was going to get some answers. I told him the whole story from the beginning. He didn't say much; he just listened.

"Thank you for contacting us. I'll get back with you when I find something out," he said.

"Thank you so much," I said, unable to hold back my happiness. Someone with power was going to help me. I wondered if they'd contact the command and if they would know I filed a congressional. Of course I knew that they would, but when?

Months passed. I experienced the same old things, day in and day out. Every sixth day, I had watch. On every work day, I cleaned. If it rained, I learned how to sweep water puddles with a straw broom on a non-skid surface. The more it rained, the more the puddles filled with water, and the more I had to sweep trying to move the water. Doing so took talent, a talent that I didn't possess. Of course, that was probably because I wasn't motivated. All I needed was a fist pump.

Since I hadn't heard from Wayne at Congressman Stewart's office, I decided to give him a call. There was no answer. My call went straight to voice mail. I left a message asking them to please give me a call back. Days passed and my call was not returned. I thought I'd try again. Once again, there was no answer and I left a message. I was beginning to feel discouraged. A week went by and my call was not returned. So, I tried again. This time, Wayne answered.

"Hello?" he said in his deep voice.

"This is OS3 Taylor and I was just..." He cut me off.

"Taylor, do not call here anymore. We will call you," he said very rudely and then hung up the phone.

What had just happened? I didn't even get a chance to find out what was going on. The man just hung up on me. Something was wrong.

From that day forward, Congressman Stewart's office never contacted me again. I believe they were told to leave the case alone. The navy was doing something to cover up what they'd done. What was it?

CHAPTER TWENTY ONE

Hardship

The last few months of working on the ship were hard. The ship had gone into dry dock to have some work done, so everyone moved to a barge. Work days were long and consisted mostly of cleaning. Most of the officers on the ship didn't talk to me anymore. A few still considered me to be a slut and believed Chief Weinerbangher's stories. My reputation had been tarnished and I knew that promotion on the ship would be difficult. I also knew that no matter what command I entered in the future, my bad reputation would follow.

Since John had taken off, he didn't play an active role in Aria's life. He was too busy with Suzanne, who was a lot older than John. There was a part of me that was happy for John. I knew that he was a person that was always full of shit, but now, Suzanne was able to step forward as a mother and change his diapers and for this I was grateful to wipe my hands clean. I guess I'd not been able to provide him with the mother figure that he needed. Since John was in the marines, I realized that it was hard on Aria to have both of her parents in the service. Once the divorce was final, both John and I could be sent out on deployment at the same time. I didn't want Aria to have to go through that experience. Since John had been in the marines for thirteen years already, I thought that my best bet would be to put in a request for an early out due to a parenting hardship. This was considered an honorable discharge. I knew that the navy was also downsizing. I'd heard that they were looking to get rid of sailors in certain military occupational specialties. OS was one of those areas.

Heading down to the ops office on the barge, I went to look for OSC Tartlette. I planned to discuss my options with him. Sure enough, he was in the office doing some paperwork.

"Chief, can I talk to you for a moment?" I said assertively.

Looking up he said, "Sure. What's up?"

"Well," I started, "given the situation of my husband leaving, things have been hard on me and my daughter. It's difficult taking care of her as a single parent. My husband is in the marines and I find it unstable for my daughter at this time if and when both of us are gone. My daughter didn't take it well when her father left, and it's important to me as a parent to be there for her. I'd like to put in a package for an early out under a parenting hardship. I'm going to be putting together my package this week in order to send it off to the board for review."

He looked at me surprised and then asked, "Are you sure that's something that you want to do? I don't think they'll give you an early out. I'll let the ops office know and they'll let the CO know what you're doing. He'll probably want to talk to you. I know that he has to write a statement on the package and sign it before you can send it to the board."

"That's fine," I told him.

"OK," he said looking back down at his paperwork. I walked out of the office intending to go get started on the package.

By the end of the week, I'd completed my hardship package. The ops officer informed me that the CO wanted to speak with me. The meeting was set for 1000. *Good*, I thought to myself. *I'm getting everything done effectively.* I knew that there was a chance that my package could be denied, but I had to try. There was no harm in trying.

At 1000, I headed up to the CO stateroom. I knocked on the door and the CO told me to enter and have a seat. The ops officer was present as well as OSC Tartlette. The CO began the conversation.

"Taylor, it has come to my attention that you want to submit a package for an early out due to your daughter and her care. I don't believe it's necessary for her to receive extra care. I also don't believe that it's a hardship on you to care for your daughter. If she needs to get to school or to places after school, there are buses and public transportation to take her."

I had to chime in. "Sir, my daughter is only nine years old. I am not about to let my daughter take a bus or public transportation by herself. Not in the world that we live in today. You should know what I'm talking about because I know that you have a daughter around the same age."

I could tell he did not like my comment.

"Taylor, I don't know what to think about this. I don't know whether or not I want to write a statement and sign the paperwork. I'm 50/50, borderline, wishy washy at the moment."

This man was the CO of the ship? Seriously? He couldn't give me a straight answer. I'd never before heard someone tell me that they were borderline. I wondered if men on the front lines thought that way. That's how soldiers get killed. I wouldn't want him taking me into battle. By that time, I couldn't help but have a disgusted and confused look on my face.

"OK," he continued. "I'll write up a statement and sign it, but I'm not writing up that I think you should have an early release. I'll give it to the ops officer today and she will give it to you. Now if that is it, you can go ahead and go."

Standing up I told him, "Thank you, sir."

I didn't care what his write-up said. I still intended to submit my package.

Sure enough, the CO kept his word. That evening before I went home, I received the statement and signed paperwork. The ops officer told me to make sure and have the legal officer, LTJG

Oleander, review the package to make sure I had everything. When I was ready to send, I was told to take it down to admin to have them fax it to the board.

That evening when I got home, I thought that I'd better make copies of the package. I didn't trust anyone on the ship, especially the admin. They had a way of losing things.

The next morning, I took my complete package to LTJG Oleander. She looked everything over and told me that it looked complete and ready to send. Once I left her office, I headed down to admin. I didn't have to say a thing. They took my package, said that they would fax it, and that I could come back in an hour. They told me that since it was sixty pages, it would take them a while to send it. I told them that was fine and said I'd be back. Since Smith was on watch outside the barge, I decided to go and keep her company. The barge wasn't too busy, so it felt nice to stand outside and talk with her. There was a cool breeze in the air and the sun was shining. At times, the barge felt stuffy and hot inside.

Once my hour was up, I returned to admin to pick up my package. When I walked into the office, they handed me back the faxed package right away. I'd just have to wait to see what the board would say. I'd heard that it normally took about a week or two to hear back. Maybe things were finally going to start looking up for me.

CHAPTER TWENTY TWO

Lost

A week had gone by when I was pulled into LTJG Oleander's office.

"Taylor, we heard back from the board. They said that they're missing the page with the CO's signature. Look; I know it was in there because I saw it. Here's a printout of the paperwork that you need."

At the bottom of the paper, she'd circled a contact name, a phone number, and a fax number. She handed me the paper without saying a word. I just looked at the paper and then looked at her before walking out the door. I knew that the paper was in there. I'd seen it, too. Someone down in admin must have taken it out. I didn't even notice that it wasn't in the package when they handed the paperwork back to me. I wondered if the CO had something to do with the paperwork missing.

I planned to be one step ahead of them. I immediately went into female berthing and called my mom. I told her what had happened and asked her to do me a favor. I told her to take the copies I'd made and find a place to fax the package. I had a feeling that some papers might get lost, so, I had made copies of everything in that package. I gave her the contact name and fax number on the paper given to me by LTJG Oleander. After I called my mom, I called the lady on the contact sheet. She was very nice. I explained to her who I was and told her that I would be faxing over the package again with the missing sheet. She told me she would look out for it.

An hour later, my mom called to let me know that she'd sent the fax. She told me it was expensive, but it was worth it. Now that I knew the package had been sent, I called the woman listed as the contact once more. She told me she'd received everything and thanked me. She told me that she would submit it to the board and that I should hear something soon.

I didn't say a word to anyone on the ship about what I had done. I continued working, cleaning, and standing watch. I minded my own business. If I had said anything, I knew that something would happen to my package and they would stop it from going through. What they didn't know couldn't hurt them.

CHAPTER TWENTY THREE

Release

E xactly a week had passed since I refaxed my hardship papers. Smith and I were on watch again and were working in the ops office on a spreadsheet for the engineering officer. He was the nicest officer on the ship, so no one minded doing favors for him. Since Smith and I had significant experience working in Microsoft Excel, the engineering officer had asked us to help him create a spreadsheet to keep track of items in the engineering room. While we were busy working, the ops officer stuck her head in.

"Taylor, can I speak to you for a moment out in the p-way?"

"Yes ma'am," I answered.

The ops officer looked at me with a puzzled expression. I couldn't guess from her expression what she wanted to talk to me about. Maybe they'd found out what I'd done. She spoke quietly.

"Taylor, I heard back from the board today and they sent out your discharge papers. You have a week to be processed out of the navy. I was shocked to receive your orders."

In her hand she held my orders to be discharged. She handed them to me and told me to get with CT1 who would help sign me out.

I felt so happy. I couldn't stop smiling. Based on her reaction to the news, I could tell that she didn't understand how I'd been able to get discharged. The last that she'd heard, the paperwork signed by the CO had been lost. I ran over to Smith and told her right away. She was so happy for me. She gave me a hug. I ran to the female berthing to call my mom.

Since I only had a week to check out, I would have to work fast to get everything completed. I had to check out with medical and dental, different departments on the ship, CMC, XO, and CO, and lastly personnel support activity detachment (PSD), which is where I would receive my DD214 and turn in my ID. Medical and dental didn't take long. They signed off on my check-out sheet and handed me my medical and dental records. As I made my way around ship, I checked out with the different departments. That left three people to check out with: the CMC, XO, and CO. CT1 said that she would set up times for me to meet with them so that I wouldn't have to chase them down. She also told me that everyone who left the ship needed an exit interview with the CO.

While I waited in berthing for her to return with meeting times, I played around on my cell phone. I heard the door to berthing open and looked over to see CT1.

"Uh...Taylor? I guess there is no exit interview with you. They don't find it necessary to meet with you and don't need to sign your check-out list. That is strange."

Before she walked out, she told me that I was all done. I would just need to go to Personnel Support Detachment (PSD) in the morning. I knew why they didn't want to meet with me. I think that they were shocked to find out that I'd gotten my discharge papers and they wondered how I'd made that happen. They also didn't want to hear what I had to say. That was fine with me. I didn't care that they didn't want to talk to me. I just felt disappointed that the CO didn't even give me a fist pump. I mean that sarcastically, of course.

CHAPTER TWENTY FOUR

Light at the End of the Tunnel

My last day in the navy had finally arrived. All I had left was to go to PSD to check out. Waiting at the top of the barge for muster, I stood in line smiling, knowing it was the last muster I'd ever have to do. After muster, I went up to OSC Tartlette and told him that I needed to go to PSD to check out.

"Taylor, I've been informed that you should go to PSD after you've done cleaners. I need you to walk over to the ship to clean the OS spaces. After you've cleaned, you can go to PSD."

I knew I couldn't argue. These people were something else. They had to get at me one more time before I left the USS Russiantown. The only way they could punish me was to make me clean. Heading over to the ship, the OSs asked me what I was doing. They agreed that it was stupid that I'd been sent over to clean one last time. When I got to BFFT, I grabbed a broom. OS2 Kowlesky snatched the broom out of my hand.

"Taylor, don't be ridiculous. You are not cleaning. You'll sit here in BFFT until cleaners is over. It's ridiculous that they sent you here to clean on your last day."

I looked at him, didn't say a word, and sat down. I did what I was told. I wasn't going to argue. I must have been sitting there for thirty minutes when the door to BFFT slowly opened. It was the ops officer. I knew that she would say something because I wasn't cleaning. She shut the door and looked at me.

"So, Taylor," she said quietly. "It's your last day in the navy. Are you happy about that?"

"Yes," I replied. "I am."

"It was what you wanted. I still don't understand how you got your discharge."

I wasn't about to tell her the truth, so I answered, "I guess admin must have found the paper with the CO's signature and sent it."

She walked over to me and leaned on one of the filing cabinets.

"You know, Taylor, I thought it was ridiculous that they made you come over and clean."

With that, she opened the door and walked out. I never did see her again.

Once cleaners were over, I went straight to berthing to grab my bags. I walked down the ladder well waving good-bye to some of the friends I'd made on the ship. I opened the door to access the quarterdeck and placed my shiny, black shoe on the deck. The sun glistened in my eyes blinding me from seeing the blue sky ahead. My eyes were drawn to the shadow of a flag, visible in the ripples in the water. In a few steps and for the last time, I'd be drawing my right arm to create an angle that means both freedom and pride. I felt proud to do so.

"Permission to go ashore for the last time," I stated, enunciating each word with precision.

"Permission granted," said Petty Officer Somner rendering a salute in response to my own.

As I walked away, I couldn't help but think back on the memories, both good and bad, that I carried with me. It all seemed like a dream.

I never did find out what happened to my officer package. That will haunt me for the rest of my life. As for Chief Weinerbangher, he was discharged a few weeks after I left the navy.

The first thing I did when I got out of the navy was contact a committee designed to help women who'd fallen victim to sexual harassment in the military. I told them my story. I told them how Chief Weinerbangher never received punishment for what he'd done. He was removed from the ship and sent to work at an offshore activity. Chief Weinerbangher cost me my career and reaching my goal of becoming a naval officer.

As for John, he married Suzanne once the divorce was final. I will never forgive him for what he did, but I realize now that he actually did me a favor. I ended up dating a wonderful man named David. We'd worked together a long time ago, before I joined the navy. He was always a good friend to me. With David came two stepdaughters. Although they live in another state, it completed our new family. He is the best man I could ever ask for. I feel very lucky to have him in my life and in Aria's.

I am ready to start a whole new chapter in my life. Just when I thought that all hope was lost, hope found its way back into my life.

Lisa Hunt grew up in San Diego, California. After graduating from University City High School, she received a BA in business education. In 2007, she joined the navy. While enlisted and out to sea, her passion for writing a book began. After returning home, she continued her education and received an MBM in business management and is currently working on a master in logistics. She has a wonderful husband, one daughter, and two stepdaughters.

Made in the USA
Charleston, SC
31 January 2014